I0824127

OLD CUBA

Los Doce Apóstoles

OLD CUBA

Alicia E. García
Photos by Julio A. Larramendi

Rizzoli
New York

New York · Paris · London · Milan

In memory of a great Cuban: María Luisa Lobo Montalvo

First published in the United States of America in 2017 by
RIZZOLI INTERNATIONAL PUBLICATIONS, INC.
300 Park Avenue South, New York, NY 10010
www.rizzoliusa.com

ISBN-13: 978-0-8478-5847-7
Library of Congress Control Number: 2016952650

© 2017 Rizzoli International Publications, Inc.
Text © 2017 Alicia E. García
Translation by Alicia Grisel Padrón
Photography © 2017 Julio A. Larramendi

All rights reserved. No part of this publication may be reproduced, stored in a retrieval system, or transmitted in any form or by any means, electronic, mechanical, photocopying, recording, or otherwise, without prior consent of the publisher.

Distributed to the U.S. Trade by Random House, New York

Front endpapers: Mural within El Templete in Old Havana representing Bishop Espada's retinue during the monument's inauguration ceremony.
Back endpapers: Santísima Trinidad Main Parish Church
Page 1: Interior of 3 Máximo Gómez Street, Sancti Spíritus
Pages 2–3: View of Havana from the Morro Castle, Havana Bay
Page 4–5: Plaza Vieja, Old Havana
Page 7 (opposite): Tomás Terry Theater, Cienfuegos

Designed by Aldo Sampieri

Printed and bound in Italy

2023 2024 2025 / 10 9 8 7 6 5 4 3 2

Page 9:
José Rafael Ortiz Palace, Trinidad

Pages 12–13:
Bird's-eye view of Trinidad

CONTENTS

View of Trinidad from the bell tower of the Convent of San Francisco

INTRODUCTION

CUBA, the largest island in the West Indies, is the queen of an archipelago made up of over 1,600 small islands and cays. One of the most outstanding of these is Isla de La Juventud. Once called Isle of Pines or Treasure Island, it was a refuge for pirates in times gone by. From Cabo de San Antonio, the extreme point in the west, all the way to Maisí, the easternmost tip of the island, Cuba is 1,200 kilometers (745.6 miles) long. Its over 3,500 kilometers of coastline are famous for their beautiful bays. Many of these are pocket bays with characteristic narrow entrance channels and circular in shape, created by the sea penetrating inland at the estuary of large rivers and consequently flooding the valleys. The coastline is resplendent with fine sandy beaches and *diente de perro* cliffs alongside the array of blues of the ever-changing sea, depending on the depth of the exceptionally varied seabed. Flora and fauna typical of the tropics round out the natural beauties of the island.

Located just south of the Tropic of Cancer, Cuba dominates the entrance to the Gulf of Mexico in close proximity to the Florida and Yucatan peninsulas. It is the navel of the Americas between the North and South American continents, and a bridge between the New World and the Old. This geographical location has been a determining factor throughout its history.

Christopher Columbus' ships landed on Cuban soil on October 27, 1492. Between mid-1508 and July of 1509, Sebastián de Ocampo sailed around the island thereby proving its insularity. The conquest of Cuba was entrusted to the nobleman from Extremadura, Diego Velázquez de Cuellar (1465–1523). From that point in time until 1898, Cuba was governed by Spain. This era is known in Cuban history as the Colonial Period. This book deals with the architecture and urban growth during that period.

When the Spanish set foot on the island, the indigenous peoples (the Taínos) were in different stages of development ranging somewhere between Paleolithic and Neolithic. The Taínos were related to the Arawak from South America and were the most advanced given that they were highly skilled in agriculture and pottery, although their communities were organized as communes, lacking any concept of ownership or wealth.

Close to the most populated of these native villages, near the rivers where the Spanish set up their gold-panning sites and typically on the southern coast, the Spanish founded the first towns from 1511 to 1515: Nuestra Señora de la Asunción de Baracoa (1511), San Salvador del Bayamo (1513), Santísima Trinidad (1514), Sancti Spíritus (1514), San Cristóbal de la Habana (1514), Santa María del Puerto Príncipe (1515) and Santiago de Cuba (1515). La Sabana, later named El Cayo or San Juan de los Remedios del Cayo, which was founded in the first half of the sixteenth century, can be added to this list.

Previous pages:
Nuestra Señora del Rosario Church, on periphery of Havana Bay

This page:
Bird's-eye view of the city of Cienfuegos; in the foreground is Plaza Mayor, in the background, the Bay of Jagua

The urban model for these early towns was based on the regular rectangular grid plans of Late Medieval Spanish cities. The original nucleus of these cities was notably linear as seen in the quasi-parallelism of two or three streets to each other, much like the old cities in Spain on the Camino de Santiago. Located at one or both ends of the first Cuban towns were the native settlements, which were later assimilated into those towns' layouts.

The new cities were governed by *cabildos*, governmental bodies made up of individuals who by their residency rights received an urban lot and a rural property. Parceling therefore reflected a manner of organizing society that was supported by the notion of *vecino*, or householder, a legal concept in Late Medieval Spain. From the beginnings of the history of Spanish America, the urban representation of that form of government was the regular layout. The way that buildings were inserted into the city grid determined the compact, closed-in appearance of Spanish-Creole cities, with continuous stretches of walls along the streets. Houses were built at ground level, next to one another, based on the Mediterranean style of house with a courtyard, which was adopted in any kind of geographical climate or social circumstances from the sixteenth century up to the early twentieth century. Empty spaces or plazas were reserved for buildings having political or religious significance and for the residences of the upper class.

The formality of granting and setting up urban and rural lots was marked by great solemnity and carried out under strict ceremonial rules that recalled ancestral customs related to traditions and superstitions of ancient peoples. These kinds of practices were kept right into the eighteenth century, like the one performed by the *cabildo* of Matanzas—when a piece of land was granted, ownership of the lot was made effective when the owner ran three times around the area loudly proclaiming "This is mine!"

Toward the end of the seventeenth and most of the eighteenth centuries, the erection of parishes consolidated the existence of numerous rural settlements that sprang up spontaneously in tobacco growing lands. Some of these towns were Quivicán (1700), Bejucal (1713), Mantua (1716), Santa María del Rosario (1728), Güines (1735), Pinar del Río (1773) and Jaruco (1769), among many others. Three important cities were founded: Santa Clara (1689), Matanzas (1693) and Holguin (1720) based on foundational plans.

A colonizing explosion related to the expansion of sugar and coffee plantations took place in the eighteenth century and in the first decades of the nineteenth century. Old settlements were consolidated or new towns were created, such as the city-ports of Guantánamo (1796–1803), Manzanillo (1794–1809), Sagua la Grande (1812), Gibara (1817), Cienfuegos (1819), Nuevitas (1775–1828), Cárdenas (1828) and Caibarién (1819–1832). Exponents of the best urban planning of the times, these cities are characterized by a strictly orthogonal layout, and some feature lovely avenues bordered by porticos that enhance the cities of the Enlightenment.

In the nineteenth century, most of Cuba's cities acquired the architectural style that distinguishes them today given the reiteration of certain building resources. This accentuated the environmental uniformity that identifies the historical centers, featuring examples of military, religious, domestic and civil architecture, which along with the building occurring in the rural areas, make up Cuba's valuable architectural heritage of the sixteenth to the nineteenth centuries.

With the exception of military fortifications, we are dealing with traditional architecture, although some outstanding examples of religious, civil or domestic buildings reveal both the talent of illustrious builders and the intent by master builders to create relevant works. Consequently, when we mention features influenced by historical styles, we do not propose to recognize the contributions of such trends, but rather to distinguish elements of form adopted according to eras that have contributed toward characterizing local expressions. Note that "traditional" does not mean any lack of originality, let alone a lack of identity since the "new" did not originate from stylistic concerns—a bottleneck that has led to a dead end when analyzing the "American" character in architecture. The "new" came from the anthropological angle since the cultural transferences received from the Old World acquired new meanings the moment they began to function in different geographical and social milieus.

As we have already pointed out, Spanish-American urban planning and architecture were based on two models coming from Spain: regular city grids and houses with inner courtyards. In Spain, however, the direction taken by each of these elements occurred separately—regular medieval cities did not necessarily have homes with inner courtyards, and the cities with irregular plans, if they were of Muslim influence, were predominantly made up of houses with inner courtyards. In Spanish America, however, right from its arrival, the regular street plan fused with the courtyard-house into one single element: the very new and unique city of the New World.

MARITIME FORTIFICATIONS

The defense of the Port of Havana, Spain's imperial frontier in the Americas, was a long-lived enterprise. Throughout the first three colonial centuries, two well-defined and characterized defensive systems were designed and built: the first one, from the end of the sixteenth century up to the mid-eighteenth century; the second one, in the second half of the eighteenth century.

In January of 1586, the English privateer Sir Francis Drake attacked the cities of Cartagena de Indias (Colombia) and Santo Domingo (Dominican Republic). This catastrophe alerted Spain to the strategic value of its West Indian possessions. If Spain was to lose the Caribbean, it would lose all of Spanish America. In February of that year, King Phillip II commissioned the renowned Italian military engineer Bautista Antonelli (1547–1616) to construct an intercontinental defensive system of extraordinary proportions that would include the fortification of several ports in the Caribbean. The construction of these immense buildings and of the walls of many cities was one of the greatest construction feats of modern times.

Among the fortified ports, Havana was an especially important enclave—from 1561, it became the meeting place of ships crossing between the Americas and Spain loaded with riches from Mexico, Peru and other Spanish-American lands. The formidable fortresses El Morro and La Punta were erected at the entrance to Havana Bay. Both were significant examples of military construction art of the sixteenth and seventeenth centuries. Defense works were also built along the Havana coastline to complement the ones in the port. Part of this first defense system is the San Severino Castle in the Bay of Matanzas, a territory considered to be the rearguard of the country's capital, coming in by land.

The second defensive system was in response to the British attack on Havana in May of 1762 carried out by a fleet of 53 ships and 25,000 men under the command of General George Keppel, 3rd Earl of Albemarle, and Admiral George Pocock. In August of that same year, the British managed to take the city, but in July of the following year, Havana was returned to Spain in exchange for Florida. The Spanish Crown then got ready to turn Havana into an impregnable city. Military engineer Silvestre Abarca (1707–1784) was appointed director of the new impressive works that included the La Cabaña Fortress, the largest one of its kind built by Spain in its empire, the Príncipe and the Atarés castles.

In both periods, building these imposing structures involved the investment and circulation of huge sums of money and bringing in engineers, master stonemasons and capable laborers. This constituted one of the mainstays for the development of architecture. Antonelli and Abarca arrived with their retinues of professionals who not only worked on the military commissions, including the city walls, but also participated in city planning and building. The fortresses were "schools of architecture" that made it possible to acquire mastery over stone, mortar and wood, as well as the skills to deal with difficult challenges in the area of building. This is part of the reason why Havana attained such a splendid urban and architectural developmednt.

Another reason that motivated the building of fortifications was combating smuggling, an activity that prospered during the seventeenth and early eighteenth centuries. A large number of castles, small forts and bastions were built to protect inlets, rivers and coastlines all over the island. The fear that the enemy would capture part of the island's territory resulted in the construction of some of the most outstanding fortresses, such as the Morro Castle in Santiago de Cuba, the Matachín Fort in Baracoa and the Jagua Castle in Cienfuegos.

RELIGIOUS BUILDINGS

During the colonial period, the Church was a highly significant player on the social scene, above all because of the genuinely religious feelings in society, but also because the Spanish Crown had received the *Patronato Real*, or royal patronage, from the Pope, head of the Roman Catholic Church. This meant that the Spanish monarchs had the power to name members of the clergy and subordinate the building of churches to the approval and control of the State. In the Spanish territories, Church and State formed a political-ideological unit. The activities carried out by of the religious orders were added to those of the secular clergy. Church members had great importance in the planning of cities, in the adoption of certain solutions in building and in the development of the era's material and spiritual culture.

In terms of city planning, the location of parish churches determined the center of the cities. This would be the starting point for the cities' layout and growth. In front of the church, an open space was left for the Plaza Mayor, or main square. To live near the cathedral was a source of great consolation and pride for our grandmothers. The lives of the colonial populations were guided and organized by the church bells. The location of the main parish church was also the physical reference point for measuring the municipal jurisdictions.

In the case of Cuba, churches and convents belonging to the male religious orders would be located in close proximity to the main parish church and the Plaza Mayor. The streets connecting the parish churches to the Franciscan and Dominican churches became the main city arteries. Routes used for the processions organized by the Franciscans during Holy Week were transformed into arterial roads within the urban fabric.

Early churches were located at the side of their squares, so the entrances could be accessed from the side doorways. This peculiarity may stem from the process used in Spain to transform mosques into churches, since the former were generally entered on their long sides as were the

Opposite:
A streetscape in Trinidad

Pages 28–29:
The Sierra Maestra with Morro Castle, Santiago de Cuba, at right

Roman basilicas that inspired them. But it could also be a throwback to the medieval custom of opening the front doors only on special festivities for the monarchs, nobility and ecclesiastical dignitaries to pass through. No matter the reason, the first Cuban towns still have churches that are located according to sixteenth- and seventeenth-century customs. Cuban churches began to switch their façades towards the squares in the eighteenth century, a tardy adoption of the precepts defended by the Counter-Reformation of the first half of the sixteenth century.

Churches built with solid materials were relatively late in comparison with other Spanish-American territories since such materials began to be used in the seventeenth century. The few churches in sixteenth-century Cuba were simple structures made of *embarrado* (mud, vegetable fiber and sticks) or wood, with *guano* (dried royal palm leaves) thatched roofs. The first stone and mortar, rammed earth or brick parish churches were modest expressions of Spanish-Mudéjar building traditions, the work of anonymous master builders/architects. These churches followed the building system stipulated by the Building Ordinances of Seville of 1527, a true Mudéjar building code whose principles go even further back in time. These ordinances were adopted by the Havana *cabildo* at the beginning of the seventeenth century.

Under the ordinances, masons and bricklayers had to know how to build three-nave churches with columns and arches, wooden or vaulted roofs—the basic type used for early Cuban churches. They often had only a single nave but in all cases the apse would be part of the rectangle defined by the naves or as an extension of them, always arranged in a square and framed by a great triumphal arch, either rounded or three-hinged, and sometimes built of wood. The side naves were connected by rounded arches held up by columns on rectangular bases or wooden posts.

The roof of the single or the central nave, depending on the case, consisted of a wooden framework with two, three or four hip ends, braced with reinforced hip rafters at the corners with angle braces. It was usual to highlight the tie beams with tracery thereby forming one of the main decorative elements in these ceilings, as well as the geometrical carved or painted wood decorations.

The façades were extremely simple with doorways accentuated by Mudéjar-Herrerian inspired decorations, like spandrels with rounded or segmental arches in the access bays, often with pilasters topped with pointed capitals, and overhanging eaves or rowlocks to finish off the walls. Initially, churches had simple belfries which were replaced or complemented by tower bells attached to one side of the façade.

Churches with greater architectural aspirations were being built during the eighteenth century. Those involved in their construction were builders who called themselves "architects," clerics with training in architecture and military engineers. Special mention should be made of the remarkable group of Havana churches that display baroque influence. These one- or three-nave churches were built from local shelly limestone and had vaulted ceilings, although some continued to display a preference for wooden roofs. The best features of these monuments were focused on the retable-façades, complete with undulating lines. The towers were monumental. The interiors were splendidly outfitted with gold-laminated retable-altars, or reredoses, some of which have survived to our day. Also to be noted are pulpits, choirs, balustrades, religious images, paintings, objects made of silver and other metals, vases and linen.

Convents were significant for both urban and architectural reasons, occupying large areas with their hulking volumes. The early ones to be built in Havana, such as the first version of the San Francisco Convent and the convent for the sisters of Santa Clara were the principal transmitters of Spanish-Mudéjar building traditions with their wooden framework ceilings, rammed earth walls and other architectural solutions that are a part of said tradition. The convents built or remodeled in the eighteenth and nineteenth centuries generally had cloister courtyards surrounded by galleries held up by wooden posts or arch-roofed passageways supported by columns.

Nineteenth-century churches adopted the neoclassical style with their façades set off by entablatures, cornices, canopies, corbels, columns or pilasters, while their austere interiors exhibited vaulted or wooden roofs. Sometimes the walls were enhanced by mural decorations. The large towers on one or both sides, or in the center, all point to the significance these churches had for the cities, besides the fact that some of them were remarkably big. The façades were oriented toward the squares, and often the churches were placed right in the middle of the squares, which then became recreational parks.

Neo-Gothic inspired buildings appeared at the end of the nineteenth century. The Gothic Revival, or Neo-Gothic, style continued to be successful through the first decades of the twentieth century in both Catholic and Protestant churches built of masonry, stone or wood.

CIVIC BUILDINGS

Civic buildings are destined for administrative, political, cultural, recreational or social functions. In early centuries, these types of buildings were not predominant since efforts were mainly concentrated on producing fortifications and churches. At any rate, civic buildings were being built from the very beginning of the Spanish colonization.

The oldest example is Diego Velázquez's fort-residence in Santiago de Cuba, the island's first capital. Built from 1520 to 1523 to serve as the governor's residence, it included embrasures in keeping with his position and the era, and could have been associated with the Casa de Fundición del Oro, the gold foundry. Also from the sixteenth century is the defensive tower adjunct to the customs building, subsequently incorporated with the Pedroso House in Havana.

Also in Havana, various structures of the old Zanja Real or aqueduct are still standing. Built by Bautista Antonelli in the late sixteenth century, it was successively lengthened in later years. Buildings for the *cabildo*, jail, butcher shop, slaughter-house, fish and other markets were built in accordance with their specific characteristics.

However, during the first three centuries of the colonial period, it was common to see civic functions being housed in domestic structures as was the case in the late sixteenth century of installing the Havana *cabildo* in the former home of Captain Francisco de Moncayo, which was also adapted to serve as jail. Stores or artisan establishments would often be located on the ground floors of residential buildings. Such spaces were also used as warehouses for products from plantations, while mezzanines were used for offices.

Seventeenth-century homes in Havana included accessory rooms that would connect directly to the street as accommodations for individuals waiting for months at a time for passage on the Fleet of the Indies ships headed for Spain. A number of houses were outfitted as schools, such as the San Francisco de Sales School, established in the late seventeenth century in a very old house at No. 4 Oficios Street; as hospitals; and as various other community services. Multi-functionality was a common feature for houses of the era.

In the late eighteenth century, Havana saw the first civic buildings, whose architectural plans were subordinated to their end use. Worth mentioning are the militia headquarters, the principal theater, the San Lázaro Hospital, the San Isidro Hospice, the orphanage, the general post office and the Palacio de los Capitanes Generales.

Civic buildings, however, became more important after 1818, the year when free trade was approved, thereby removing the obstacles that were slowing down the island's economic development, which rested basically on the promotion of sugar and coffee plantations. This is the time when Cuban cities acquired a full-fledged urban appearance due to the paving of the streets, putting in sidewalks, installing water and lighting systems, and building parks and boulevards embellished with fountains and commemorative monuments. All sorts of buildings serving specific purposes were making their appearance: city halls, customs buildings, warehouses, docks, lighthouses, markets, hospitals, jails, garrisons,

theatres, lyceums, schools, train stations, botanical gardens, bridges, highways, cemeteries, factories, pharmacies and many other of different kinds.

It is to be noted that the railway, which was established from 1834 to 1837, was one of the vehicles for introducing the most modern architectural and technological solutions related to the use of iron, wood and the updating of neoclassical and eclectic styles. The railroad transformed Cuba's geography, bringing together the most remote areas and connecting them to shipping points, definitively modifying the country through the building of the associated infrastructure. The space-time relationship had attained a new meaning.

Urban planning and organization was being submitted to stricter controls in accordance with the stipulations of municipal ordinances—legal codes that determined how cities functioned and the forms of their buildings. Works were taken over by outstanding Spanish, Cuban, or international builders. Also playing its part was the Cuba Corps of Engineers, whose personnel mastered the academic rules of building and the most modern technical solutions available at the time.

Cuba is indebted to those engineers and builders for the architectural projects of the buildings, the layouts for new cities and the expansion of old ones; the studies and implementation of urban networks and railway lines, including associated structures, the survey of bays and the construction of docks, warehouses and other facilities; territorial studies related to land and sea communications and to the promotion of agriculture on the island. This monumental task can be seen in the architectural and engineering drawings that constitute a valuable cartographic asset that is safeguarded in archives and libraries in Cuba and Spain.

HOUSES

The reference model for Cuban domestic architecture is the house-with-inner-courtyard layout, whose configuration depended on locations and time periods. In this regard, Havana played a significant role as the central propagator of models imported from the metropolis. The oldest large homes in Havana were built of rock, rammed earth or masonry and followed the Spanish-Mudéjar style that was characterized by an entrance doorway leading into a rectangular courtyard surrounded by galleries supported on wooden posts on one or several sides. Usually two-storied, the rooms on the ground level would be used, as mentioned above, for public functions and the upper floor would be reserved for the dwelling per se. In the late seventeenth century, a new type of home, also of the Mudéjar type, made its appearance, placing the entrance doorway to the side of the façade. This is the model that developed into Havana's longstanding, one-story *casa-zaguán* (house with large vestibule).

The façades of very important houses had wooden balconies, a structure whose development coincides with the conquest and colonization of Spanish America. Therefore, this element became one of the identifying features of architecture in the region. The wooden balcony is the Mudéjar version of the refined models made of stone that were in fashion from the time of the Renaissance. In earlier centuries, they were an attribute of social significance just like the towers that allowed looking out over the sea. In the interiors, the parlors and other important rooms were covered with typical frameworks with tracery patterns.

Stately homes called *señoriales* were being built during the first decades of the eighteenth century. These two-story houses with mezzanine were distributed around a square-shaped inner courtyard surrounded by arched galleries held up by columns. The main rooms maintained the preference for wooden ceilings. Spacious wooden balconies stretched along the façades and the entrance doorways were resplendently baroque. Built facing the squares, these mansions incorporated portals on the ground floor and loggias on the second.

For a long time, in provincial towns, homes were simple structures made of wood or earth and *guano* roofs. Examples of lean-to houses, that is, having a roof with a single slope, still survive in eastern Cuba. These types of houses were widespread in the early centuries all over the country, including Old Havana. The early eighteenth century saw the appearance of the first houses made of masonry, bricks or rammed earth. They were typically one-story houses characterized by big wooden grilles, overhanging eaves or rowlocks, log ceilings in the simpler homes or framework with tracery in the more elegant ones.

Toward the last third of the eighteenth century and in the first decades of the nineteenth century, popular motifs inspired by Andalusian baroque endowed homes with a light outward appearance. Eaves with brackets, front doors with ogee or mixtilineal arches decorated with pilasters topped with goblets, lobed and mixtilineal arches, star-shaped tracery adorning the beams, and walls covered with rococo and Louis XVI–style murals became widespread in the towns of central Cuba. It was during this period that it was common to see two-story homes in the provinces, with wooden balconies and corridors attached to the façades of those built above street-level. Santiago de Cuba has the best examples of both of these then new features.

Trinidad's architecture took a giant leap forward during 1825–1830 when its jurisdiction became an important sugar growing enclave. A new room appeared on the scene: the *saleta*, which communicated with the *sala* (parlor) through great rounded arches. The dining room was moved to the gallery. The courtyard was surrounded by one or several galleries and the kitchen got placed toward the back with its hood and stove. The courtyard was paved, becoming a garden with plants growing in flowerbeds and pots. Cisterns for catching and storing rainwater from the roof gutters were built under the courtyards.

The new *sala-saleta* relationship, which had its counterpart in the neoclassical American two-parlor layout, moved to other cities in the central and eastern parts of Cuba, including Gibara, notable for the elegance of its architecture. The *casa-zaguán* with its entranceway on one side of the house, spread to the central-western region. In older towns, such as Sancti Spíritus or Remedios, or in some of the newer ones like Cienfuegos, the *casa-zaguán* interacted with the *sala-saleta* type. Cienfuegos has outstanding examples of nineteenth-century architecture, in which old traditions merge with new spatial and ornamental solutions announcing the transformations that would take place in the early twentieth century.

Both types of houses adopted several innovations of the time: stained-glass or fan-shaped shutters in the rounded arches, fan-shaped louvered doors and glass screens. All of these elements interacted with the strong tropical light and the need for allowing the breezes to pass through the houses. Other shared preferences were the love of murals and the use of cast iron. The compositions of the façades, however, were very different between the old towns and the newly founded cities. In the former, the façade walls were smooth with the occasional attached pilasters, the eaves were traditional and the sloping roof was covered by earthenware tiles. In the latter, façades were academically structured with pilasters, cornices, entablatures, parapets and classically composed portals. In the case of Havana, the houses along the main avenues outside the city walls were fronted by continuous porches; this can also be seen in some of the provincial towns, for example in Paseo del Prado Avenue in Cienfuegos. Repeating elements and similar volumes gave way to an architectural unity that typified the atmospheres in the new cities where homes formed a whole along straight streets that seemed to go on forever.

In the mid-nineteenth century, a new type of house made its appearance in the outlying neighborhoods being created as a result of urban expansion. This is the *casa-quinta*, villa or chalet featuring compact ground plans minus courtyards, entrance porticos and separated from other houses by gardens. Built of masonry, brick, stone or wood, this type of house showed early signs of eclecticism, a stylistic trend that predominated in the early twentieth century when the *casa-quinta* reached full development.

OLD HAVANA

The town of San Cristóbal de la Habana became a rich enclave thanks to its port, which had become the chief connection between the Old World and the New World. The geographical uniqueness of the capital of Cuba is derived precisely from its marine setting. Havana opens out to the sea along an extensive coastline and its original nucleus found shelter in the peninsula that penetrates its extraordinary bay, with its very narrow entrance and spacious inner pocket.

It is one of the oldest cities in the Americas. But unlike other venerable Latin American cities, whose early centers have successively undergone changes, Old Havana has preserved a traditional urban and architectural appearance with very few intrusions of modern elements.

Initially limited to the vicinity of Plaza de Armas, the town grew along the immediate edge of the bay on a long, narrow strip where the chief public buildings were located: the church, buildings belonging to religious orders, the *cabildo* (town council) and customs. By 1587, despite depending heavily on the port and in accordance with a long-simmering impulse, Plaza Nueva (now Plaza Vieja) became urbanized southwards. This new square was used as a market and for public celebrations, thereby replacing Plaza de Armas due to its military activities.

However, Amargura and Teniente Rey streets connected Plaza de San Francisco with Plaza Humilladero, later called Plaza del Cristo, turning the city's growth to an east-west direction. This change would mark the trend of its future growth past the city walls that enclosed the original town nucleus. To the north, a swampy area was filled in and turned into the plaza for the most important church in the city and one of the most significant and beloved in the country: Havana Cathedral. This laid out the old city's system of plazas to which small squares (*plazoletas*) were added to front its numerous churches and convents. In the eighteenth, nineteenth and early twentieth centuries, the construction of long-lasting buildings made the urban fabric grow denser, thus configuring the valuable city we see today, which is flanked by the sea that is also a part of its urban landscape.

Because of its exceptional architectural heritage, on December 14, 1982, UNESCO's Intergovernmental Committee for the Protection of the World Cultural and Natural Heritage declared Old Havana and its Fortifications a World Heritage Site.

Opposite:
Nuestra Señora de Belén Church

CASTILLO DE LA REAL FUERZA

1558–1577

Museo Castillo de la Real Fuerza

Bartolomé Sánchez, Engineer; Francisco de Calona, Master Builder

The Castillo de la Real Fuerza was the first Renaissance fortress to be built in the Americas. It consists of a square building divided into nine equal parts, while the central part is open to the sky in the form of a courtyard. Bulwarks stand on each corner above the moat that surrounds the entire building. In 1632, a watchtower was added and topped with a bronze statue sculpted in the form of a woman by Master Jerónimo Pinzón. The figure is called *La Giraldilla* and is considered to be one of the symbols of the city.

The ancient castle walls guarded the silver and gold of ships coming from Veracruz and Cartagena de Indias, anchored in Havana Harbor waiting to sail back to Spain together.

PALACIO DE LOS CAPITANES GENERALES

1776–1791

Museo de la Ciudad

Antonio Fernández Trevejos, Engineer; Pedro de Medina, Architect

The Palacio de los Capitanes Generales (former residence of the Captains General) is the most outstanding example of civil architecture in Old Havana. It was part of an ambitious project to remodel the square under Governor Felipe de Fonsdeviela, Marquis de la Torre (1771–1776), but only this palace and the post office, both in similar style, were built.

It is a magnificent building that follows the plan for seigniorial mansions. The first level covers the mezzanine intended for public functions and the second level was reserved for the private chambers of the island governors. The façade openings (see following pages) are framed with the peculiar mixtilineal jambs of the port cities in southern Spain, known here as "jamba habanera," or Havana jambs. It is a turn-of-the-century building that shows a combination of declining baroque and nascent neoclassicist elements, as seen in the robust pillars holding up the portico arches, which enhance the main façade.

In the center of the majestic courtyard (see previous pages) surrounded by galleries that are held up by columns with arches is the statue of Admiral Christopher Columbus sculpted by J. Cuchiari and placed there in 1862.

El Templete

1828

Antonio María de la Torre, Architect

This monument commemorating the founding of Havana was one of the first to use neoclassicist elements. The interior holds canvases by the French painter Jean Baptiste Vermay (1784–1833) depicting scenes alluding to the founding mass, to members of the Havana *cabildo* and to the ceremony inaugurating the building.

Early Havana homes were markedly trabeated with very low ceilings; precise edges and geometric compositions; and pronounced contrasts given the chiaroscuro of the shadows and the light projected by the overhanging eaves, the carvings on their roofs, the lime-coated walls and the burnt sienna tones of its cedar armatures, the "parrot green" doors and the intense colors of the clay roof tiles.

TENIENTE REY (AT THE CORNER OF AGUIAR)

Seventeenth Century/1720–Nineteenth Century

Old Havana saw the appearance of a type of dwelling whose front door was positioned at the far end of the façade, on a broken axis line with a courtyard that had no galleries on the long sides. This arrangement is reminiscent of Moslem houses in the Spanish city of Granada. A corner shop with a wooden balcony—a typical structure seen in Caribbean city-ports—was attached to the side.

OBRAPÍA (AT THE CORNER OF SAN IGNACIO)

Ca. 1650

The front door of this house faces a courtyard with galleries held up by wooden posts on several of its sides. This is typical of Spanish-Mudéjar houses known as "a la castellana."

PLAZA VIEJA

1559/1585, Seventeenth and Eighteenth Centuries

Plaza Vieja was laid out on a rectangular ground plan according to the golden ratio principle. From early years, it was exclusively civil in nature and the seigniorial residences on its perimeter had entrance porches on their façades that had been authorized by the *cabildo* as part of public areas and as city property. Loggias were situated above the porches. The result is urban-architectural testimony to the repercussion of Renaissance forms in our lands.

ARTE
CUBANO
CONTEMPORANEO

1912

EIGHTEENTH-CENTURY MANSIONS

Mansions, also known as house-warehouses, were a feature pertaining to a growing social class: the local oligarchy that had attained their wealth through trade and agriculture. Their residences had palatial pretentions, revealing an unusual dialogue among stone walls, Florentine arcades and baroque portals with Mudéjar-style wooden roofs. The doors were carved with baroque motifs, featuring curves that were refashioned in the most intricate rococo. Vestibule arches became fragmented into lobed or mixtilineal versions, or allowed hanging volutes from their keystones, which was very highly regarded by Havana architecture. The focus of the façades fell on balconies along the entire breadth of the building and on baroque adornments that set off the entryways.

Opposite:

OBRAPÍA (AT THE CORNER OF MERCADERES)

Ca. 1665–1785

Casa de la Obrapía

In 1669, this house was associated with a charity foundation that granted poor young women dowries to either get married or enter a convent. The coat of arms over the portal belongs to the Castellón family since the Obrapía patrons were obliged to use that surname. The crown above it corresponds to the title of the Marquisate of Cárdenas de Monte Hermoso.

The building was remodeled when it belonged to Gabriel de Cárdenas y Santa Cruz (1759–1815), 2nd Marquis of Cárdenas de Monte Hermoso, founder of the town of San Antonio de los Baños. The old mansion was transformed into the most outstanding baroque palace in Havana. The side entrance was opened and an extraordinary portal, which is distinguished for its Cadiz-inspired baroque details, was attached. The courtyard (see previous pages) was remodeled to have arched galleries supported by columns on three of its sides and the monumental staircase was then built.

56 AMARGURA STREET

Nineteenth Century

Mural decorations were the principal elements used to highlight the interiors of houses in this period. In some cases, they exhibited motifs inspired by the Andalusian baroque we have so often referred to and which was inclined to use forms from the Moslem past, such as mixtilineal and ogee profiles, and tracery-like strokes.

BAROQUE CHURCHES

The body of Havana churches and convents built in the eighteenth century and the first half of the twentieth century form a brilliant chapter in the history of Cuban architecture.

NUESTRA SEÑORA DE BELÉN CHURCH

1712–1718/1720

This church was built by monks from Guatemala where the Order of Bethlemite Brothers had been created in the mid-seventeenth century to help the poor. In those days there were close ties between Havana and the Captaincy General of Guatemala, belonging to the Viceroyalty of New Spain. The retable-style façade is similar to churches in the Guatemalan city of Antigua, with a great shell in the middle holding sculptures in the round representing the Nativity. This church was the first to have a stone-vaulted roof.

CONVENT OF NUESTRA SEÑORA DE BELÉN

1718–Nineteenth Century

Oficina de Asuntos Humanitarios de la Oficina del Historiador

The cloister of the convent along with the church and hospital were the original structures of the building, constructed thanks to a generous donation by Juan Francisco Carballo, a rich Havana merchant. In the mid-eighteenth century, Bishop Pedro Morell de Santa Cruz stated that the cloister had stone arches. It is therefore likely to have been one of the city's first courtyards surrounded by arched galleries held by columns. In the second half of the nineteenth century, it acquired its final appearance when the building was taken over by the reestablished Society of Jesus.

SAN FRANCISCO DE ASÍS BASILICA

1719–1738

Sala de Conciertos and Museo de Arte Sacro

The original San Francisco Church and Convent were damaged by hurricanes and reconstruction had to be undertaken. The new moderate baroque-style church, with choir stall, is impressive. The retable façade is composed of Tuscan half-columns on tall bases and crowned with serpentine profiles. The main door is crowned by a great, thick, conch-shaped arch because an impressive 42-meter bell tower was built over the central body of the building, becoming the highest elevation in the city for centuries.

The church has three naves. The central nave's barrel vaults are held up by mighty cruciform columns, illuminated by lunettes with their corresponding oculi flanked by pilasters. The floor plan is Latin-cross-shaped and the crossing was once covered by an eight-partite dome. The side naves are roofed with groin vaults.

Given that the new church was built on the same lot of the original one, it kept the same orientation to the side of the square. For that reason, one of the side naves is visible with its baluster column parapet and the undulating line of the lunettes. A doorway with its corresponding portal allows entry to the church from the square.

HAVANA CATHEDRAL

1748–1777

Havana Cathedral has been considered to be the most significant and attractive baroque monument in Cuba. Authorities on the subject agree that its famous façade shows two stages on an initial plan: a first stage when the main walls and part of the façade were erected, and a second stage when the façade and roofs were completed and the towers were added. The serpentine façade is similar to the monuments inspired by the work of the Italian architect Francesco Borromini, although styles that derive from Mexican baroque are also evident, such as polygonal arches, eight-partite towers and serpentine pediments. The Andalusian master Pedro de Medina left his signature in the swirling lines of the cornice separating the lower from the upper level, the jambs in the openings and the façade's mixtilineal crowning elements.

The building was begun in 1748 to serve as a church for the Jesuits. But the religious order was expelled from the Spanish colonies in 1767 and therefore construction work was interrupted. In 1772 it was planned to be used as the main parrish church and work recommenced, terminating shortly thereafter. In 1789, the church was elevated to the rank of cathedral.

At the start of the nineteenth century, Bishop Juan Díaz de Espada y Landa carried out extensive reforms, some of which included replacing the baroque altars with neoclassical ones, laying marble pavements and decorating the walls with paintings by the French artist Jean Baptiste Vermay. From 1957 to 1960, it was once again object of great transformations. For the visit of Pope Francis I in September of 2015, the cathedral was painstakingly restored.

NUESTRA SEÑORA DE LA MERCED CHURCH

End of the Eighteenth Century

This beautiful church was completed along baroque lines by the end of the eighteenth century after long years of hard work. Nevertheless, it remained unfinished because it was not possible to build the towers, which, on both sides of the central church body, emphasized the marked vertical accent in the design of the façade. The Lourdes Chapel, finished in 1876, was decorated by Cuban artists; some of the most outstanding were Esteban Chartrand, Miguel Melero and Pidier Petit. The walls of the naves were lavishly decorated by celebrated painters such as Jaime Comena, Francisco Planella, Francisco Piera and Manuel Lorenzo.

In the twentieth century, this church acquired great popularity among Havana residents of different social strata and it became the setting for some celebrated weddings. Dedicated to the Virgin of Mercy, it has inspired the devotion of those who identify the Virgin with the Yoruba deity Obatalá.

Many attributes allow us to recognize typical nineteenth-century houses. But the presence of forged or cast iron elements is the indicator par excellence of the era. Iron can be seen in windows, in the rounded arches, in supporting members, in balcony closures and railings, in the spectacular *guardavecinos* (grillwork separating neighbors' balconies), in the *guardacantones* (stone posts placed on the corners of houses to protect them from vehicles), in lamps and lampposts with marked classical designs: frets, ovals, lyres, arrows, rounded arches, urns…. Add to that the renewing elements of classically composed portals with pediments or entablatures held up by pilasters, canopies on corbels in the openings, framed stretches of walls with ornamental borders or pilasters, projecting cornices and the unchanging crowning parapets with glazed ceramic urns or those made of other materials, and the unroofed balconies held up by large granite pieces projecting towards the street.

The interiors clearly show the intention to avoid complicated or contrasting edges so that a harmonious, flowing and brilliant ensemble could be achieved. The first impression is considerable luminosity attained by the imposing scale and expanse of light, having replaced the old ceilings of Mudéjar armatures with flat wooden-beamed roofs known as *losa por tabla*, often covered by the ceilings. Multi-colored light filters through magnificent stained-glass rounded arches, one of the best achievements of Colonial-era Cuban architecture. The color splashing over the walls lightens the mood, as it covers the entire area from baseboards to the top of mural paintings (sometimes present in the façades) whose decorative friezes compensate for the smooth, sober architectural treatment of the walls. Smooth doors also eschew the carvings of the eighteenth century and show rectangular panels. Glistening marble floors replace dark clay pavements. Finally, the courtyard becomes the chief ornamental feature of the house with fountains, sculptures, benches, flowerbeds and trees.

These were different kinds of houses despite the fact that they barely changed the planimetric layout of their predecessors. They are genuinely elegant and lavishly outfitted seigniorial mansions.

CONDE DE VILLANUEVA PALACE

1770/Nineteenth Century

Hotel Conde de Villanueva,

Galería Julio Larramendi

JOAQUÍN GÓMEZ PALACE

Ca. 1838

Hotel Florida

Nineteenth-century Havana was considered to be the best Spanish city in the Americas because of the opulence of its buildings. Some of these were the mansions commissioned by sugar barons, industrial or business tycoons. Banker Joaquín Gómez's residence set a fashionable precedent among wealthy Habaneros. It is undeniably one of the most significant examples of the era. When it was inaugurated, its value was estimated at 100,000 pesos.

In 1916, the Florida Hotel was installed on the premises of the building and it was in business until 1950. When the building was salvaged in 1996–2000, it maintained both the name and its function as a hotel.

HOME OF SANTIAGO C. BURNHAM

1817/1882

Casa Simón Bolívar

PERIPHERY OF HAVANA BAY

The east shore of Havana Bay is part of the urban landscape of the original nucleus of the city. Close to the entrance channel, Morro Castle and La Cabaña Fortress rise majestically. Old towns like Guanabacoa (1554), and the fishing villages of Regla and Casablanca sprang up at the far end of the bay. Further inland, the town of Santa María del Rosario was founded in 1732.

Previous pages:

MORRO CASTLE

1589–1630

Parque Histórico-Militar Morro-Cabaña

Bautista Antonelli, Architect

Antonelli took advantage of the heights flanking the entrance to Havana Bay for the placement of this formidable castle. The castle becomes part of the topography of the high promontory that serves as its base. Its shape is an irregular polygon with three bulwarks joined by curtain-walls and a casemated garrison. The fortress's interior had everything it needed to withstand a prolonged siege: two large wells, a church, quarters for officers and troops, offices, dungeons and vaulted rooms. Large cannons provided the defense highlighted by a battery known as the Twelve Apostles.

Right:

LA CABAÑA FORTRESS

1763–1774

Parque Histórico-Militar Morro-Cabaña.

M. de Valliére and Silvestre Abarca, Engineers; Pedro de Medina, Architect

Constructed at a cost of 14,000,000 pesos, measuring 700 meters long and covering 10 hectares, this was the largest fortification to be built by the Spanish in the Americas. It is designed on an irregular polygon with curtain walls protected by bulwarks, towers, ravelins and bastions. It served as a prison and for executions from the colonial era until it was converted into a museum.

Left:

SANCTUARY OF NUESTRA SEÑORA DE REGLA

Seventeenth Century/1811–1818

In the early years of the nineteenth century, the old seventeenth-century church was remodeled by engineer Pedro Abad Villarreal following the canons of neoclassicism. The façade and a part of the interior are early examples of works built in that style. From 1714, the Virgin of Regla, patron of sailors and Havana Bay, is venerated in this church. Religious syncretism coupled this worship with the cult of Yemayá, goddess of the waters in the Yoruba pantheon.

ERMITA DEL POTOSÍ

1644

Guanabacoa

This old church has a rectangular façade; its corner belfry was clearly an archaic element. It was remodeled in the nineteenth century.

IHS
IHS

Left:

MAIN PARISH CHURCH OF GUANABACOA

1721

This church is noted for its wooden framework roofs and the splendid baroque altars.

Following pages:

NUESTRA SEÑORA DEL ROSARIO CHURCH

1766

Santa María del Rosario

José Perera, Architect

The Santa María del Rosario Church belongs to the family of Havana eighteenth-century religious buildings, which were influenced by a moderate baroque style. Basically, it inherited features from the earlier period: rectangular Latin cross-shaped floor plan with the bell tower to one side. But they are "modern" churches, in that their façades adopt the retable layout so frequently seen in Spanish America.

The ground level of Santa María's façade has double columns, thereby reinforcing the impression of strength, but lightened by the three-lobed crowning element on the mixtilineal pediment, with volutes. These were often used in Spanish American churches, in cultured or popular versions, based on those of the Church of the Gesú in Rome. In the middle and on the second level was the choir door, an element deriving from and replacing the medieval entrances. The Santa María Church tower is restrained and Herrerresque but still has greater weight and volume than the earlier towers of the seventeenth century.

In contrast to the baroque examples in Old Havana, the roof of this church still has the traditional wooden armature. But Santa María Church is different mainly because of its altars and their paintings, as well as the paintings in the pendentives above the transept. They were the work of Nicolás José de Escalera (1734–1804), the most outstanding Cuban painter of the eighteenth century. It has also been considered that he may have been the author of the altars. In summary, because of its architecture and interior, this is the most authentic and best conserved church in the country.

TEATRO SAUTO

MATANZAS

Matanzas was the first city to be founded in Cuba by the explicit interest of the Spanish government. It was located in a splendid geographical setting, at the back of a large bay, between two rivers and surrounded by mountains. Its foundational plan was drawn up by Juan Herrera y Sotomayor, one of the most illustrious military engineers of his time. The city was laid out in an orthogonal design and lined up with the north, had rectangular city blocks and was organized around two squares. Matanzas was quite different from other cities that had been established in Cuba and Spanish America. The cities that were akin to this one were not to be found on this side of the Atlantic, but in southern Italy in the cities built by Spain.

Those cities followed the Renaissance urban ideal that formed the basis of the Laws of Town Planning pronounced by Philip II of Spain in 1573 and incorporated into the *Recopilación de las Leyes de Indias* (Compilation of the Laws of the Indies), printed in 1681.

The history of early regular urban planning in the Americas shows three very different phases. The first of these corresponds to the early sixteenth century and develops along regular Late Medieval layouts. The second phase, taking place after the conquest of Mexico in 1523, was the *cuadrícula*, an urban model inspired by the "City of God" of Franciscan Francesc Eiximenis, and which became widespread throughout Spanish America. But the process did not end in continental territories nor did it end with the sixteenth century. The development of urban planning after 1573 had a new scenario: the Caribbean. Its leading figures, given their obvious leanings towards Renaissance theory, introduced new elements in the seventeenth century that changed the traditional plans of the cities of the region. This third "Caribbean" phase has been ignored in its specificity. Within this phase, the layout of the city of Matanzas is an essentially important milestone, an eloquent demonstration of the principles that inspired the formulation of the "ideal city" in our lands.

Classicist tendencies were added to the virtues of modern urban planning. By the mid-nineteenth century, the people of Matanzas were strolling around a city ruled by entablatures, pediments, cornices, capitals, pilasters, columns, canopies, brackets, mutules, rounded arches and other similar elements that made up a powerful architectural unit because of the repetition of themes. Such visual symphony justified calling Matanzas *The Athens of Cuba*.

Opposite:
Sauto Theater

PALACIO DE JUSTICIA

PLAZA DE LA VIGÍA

1693–Nineteenth Century

The urban layout of the city began with this square (not shown), situated between the San Juan and Yumurí rivers, apex of the triangle which comprised the original settlement. Splendid civil buildings were built in the surrounding areas.

Left:

CUSTOMS HOUSE/PALACE OF JUSTICE

1818/1828–1909/1911

Gobierno Municipal

Julio Sagebien, Architect/Remodeled in 1909–1911 by W. Armitage Ingenieros *et al*

The Customs House was considered the "cathedral" of the great sugar plantation boom, true expression of a new architectural style that emerged under the auspices of enlightened rulers. When the building was practically completed, its top floor collapsed in 1820. Its reconstruction was entrusted to the French architect Julio Sagebien, who, through this building, introduced the neoclassical style in the city. The building was later remodeled in the early twentieth century, following the eclectic canon.

SAUTO THEATER

1863

Daniel Dall'Aglio, Architect

With the construction of the theater in the center of Plaza de la Vigia, this space lost both its original ambit and the view of the sea; however, its architectural rank increased. Originally named "Esteban" in honor of Governor Pedro Esteban y Arranz (1865–1868), as of 1899, the theater was called after the surname of Ambrosio Sauto, who was the main promoter of its construction, funded through public subscription. For the construction of this work, a contest was organized and the award was accorded to the project presented by the Italian architect Daniel Dall'Aglio, who designed a building of proportions "worthy of any European capital."

Its construction posed a true challenge given the swampy ground on which its foundations were laid. As a result, a complex system of piles and wooden frameworks were built underground. Its acclaimed sonority is attributed to the foundation laying solution. Completed in 1863, the theater maintains its horseshoe layout and original appearance, and the ingenious hydraulic mechanism which elevates the orchestra to the same level as the stage, thus transforming the interior into a large ballroom. It has remained open since its inauguration. The theatre was declared a National Monument on October 10, 1978.

SAN CARLOS BORROMEO CATHEDRAL

Eighteenth–Nineteenth Centuries

After the destruction of the first church in 1730, the construction of a new parish was undertaken. Since then and up to the early twentieth century, it has been the subject of a number of additions and improvements.

PLAZA
DE LA
LIBERTAD

SAN CARLOS BORROMEO CATHEDRAL

Eighteenth–Nineteenth Centuries

After the destruction of the first church in 1730, the construction of a new parish was undertaken. Since then and up to the early twentieth century, it has been the subject of a number of additions and improvements.

PARQUE DE LA LIBERTAD

The Plaza del Rey (now Parque de la Libertad) was designed in 1764; however, execution of the project continued until 1800. This area became the most important social meeting point in Matanzas. The surrounding buildings are admirable exponents of the economic power and splendor of the second largest Cuban town in the 1800s. On February 24, 1909, the statue of José Martí was unveiled in the square. It was financed by public subscription and sculpted by the Italian artist Salvatore Bueni.

PLAZA
DE LA
LIBERTAD

Left:

GOVERNMENT HOUSE

1851–1853/1923–1931

Gobierno Provincial

Antonio Montenegro, Engineer; José Carbó, Master Builder

Above and following pages:

TRIOLET PHARMACY

1882

Museo Farmacéutico

The pharmacy owned by Ernesto Triolet remained in operation from January 1, 1882, until it became the Pharmaceutical Museum in 1964. It contains valuable objects, some of which are considered one-of-a-kind.

ERMITA DE NUESTRA SEÑORA DE MONSERRAT

1871–1875

José Bartolomé Borrell, Master Builder

This small church crowning the hill situated between the Yumurí Valley and the city was built by the wealthy Catalan community of Matanzas. The four sculptures placed in the front garden represent the Catalan provinces.

Following Pages:

SAN CARLOS BORROMEO CEMETERY

1866–1886

Juan Francisco Sánchez Bárcena, Engineer; Francisco Sosa, Master Builder; Pedro Celestino del Pandal, Architect

Sculptures, grillwork and accessories enhance the architecture of the cemetery, whose crypts below ground level are a unique reminder of the burial customs of the late nineteenth century.

SAN SEVERINO CASTLE

1693

Museo de la Ruta del Esclavo

Juan de Císcara and Juan Herrera y Sotomayor, Engineers

San Severino Castle is a remarkable example of the Renaissance fortifications erected in Cuba during the sixteenth and seventeenth centuries. They are part of the intercontinental defense system built by Spain to protect its empire in the Americas.

CÁRDENAS

Cárdenas was founded in 1828 during the expansion of the sugar industry in the west-central plains of Cuba. In just a few years, it had become a prosperous town. Laid out following a regular urban design, it was the first Cuban city to be lined up to the north-east. This represented an advantage in terms of better exposure to the sun and to the breezes. By the nineteenth century, it was architecturally consolidated, and it now exhibits a number of significant buildings from that period.

Opposite:
City Hall courtyard

Below:
Cárdenas City Hall

CITY HALL

1858–186

Museo Oscar María de Rojas, Plaza de Espriu

José Roselló Prats, Master Builder

This building stands out for its graceful portico that embellishes its façade and its ample central courtyard. An elaborate railing guards the doors crowned with stained-glass fanlights exhibiting eclectic designs inspired by neo-Gothic themes. Its spacious rooms guard and exhibit one of the most valuable museum collections in the country, including artworks and historical objects that once belonged to illustrious patriots.

560 JÉNEZ STREET

1873

Museo Casa Natal de José A. Echeverría

Bonifacio Liaño, Master Builder

This house is an excellent example of a large, two-story residence, with the entrance on one side, like a *zaguán*. The house stands out for the refinement of its components, such as ironwork, doors with blinds, stained-glass fanlights and the impressive spiral staircase made of polished mahogany wood.

PURÍSIMA CONCEPCIÓN MAIN PARISH CHURCH

1846

Manuel J. de Carrerá, Engineer

The expressive façade in the form of a small temple, with monumental Palladian-like columns similar to those in the United States, are an integral part of a structure with studied proportions and accurate symmetry. This is an epoch in which openings were designed of the same size in order to emphasize the equilibrium of the parts.

CIENFUEGOS

The Spanish Crown had long nurtured the colonization of the Bay of Jagua area. Nearby, the town of Trinidad was founded in 1514 and moved to its current location that same year. By the end of the eighteenth century, studies carried out by scientists who participated in the reconnaissance expedition of the island under Joaquín de Santa Cruz, Count of Mopox, came to the conclusion that the Majana Peninsula in the Bay of Jagua was the perfect spot to set up a town and drew up its plan in 1798. It was the perfect city for the philosophy of the Enlightenment—orthogonal, crisscrossed by portico- and tree-lined avenues leading up to a huge garden-square.

In 1819, the city of Fernandina de Jagua (today's Cienfuegos) was founded by French settlers from Bordeaux, France, and others from Spanish colonies, under the guidance of Don Luis de Clouet from Louisiana, United States of America. The city was laid out following the urban idea as set out in the 1798 plans.

In a few years, Cienfuegos became an important sugar industry center and one of the most prosperous cities in Cuba. From the mid-nineteenth century, it underwent a vigorous urban development process that enlarged the city form its original 25 blocks and saw the building of beautiful homes influenced by neoclassicism and subsequently by eclecticism. The mansions erected in the last third of the nineteenth century and in the first decades of the twentieth century are relevant examples on a national scale. Cienfuegos was a city whose urbanization was controlled by the strictly respected Construction Ordinances.

Particular care was put on the design and architectural composition of the great tree-lined avenue—Paseo del Prado—showcasing porticos on both sides. The Prado is one of the distinctive elements of Cienfuegos and one of the most attractive public areas in all of Cuba. This is the avenue that leads into the historical city. Its continuation through the peninsula on the edge of the bay gives rise to the Cienfuegos Malecón, or seafront, which allows a spectacular view of the bay. Wooden or masonry chalet-type or country houses (*quintas*) were built at the Punta Gorda neighborhood, which was developed at the far end of the peninsula. The Historical Urban Center of Cienfuegos was declared a World Heritage Site by UNESCO in 2005.

HOME OF DOMINGO SARRIA VALDESPINO

Ca. 1842–1860

Bar Palatino

Many families from the town of Trinidad arrived in Cienfuegos around 1840 seeking economic opportunities. One of those families was the Sarria family, who bought and remodeled this property. It was traditional for the houses facing the plazas to have front porches. This, however, was a unique porch in Cuba. It consisted of "potbellied' columns—rare in our milieu—similar to those of the homes in the old city of Coro, Venezuela.

PURÍSIMA CONCEPCIÓN CATHEDRAL CHURCH

1833–1869

Santiago Murray, Architect

The Cienfuegos Cathedral is an outstanding neoclassical monument. Its construction began as a simple church with a single nave. In the mid-nineteenth century, the American architect Santiago Murray remodeled the church to include three naves. The facade is enhanced by porticos in the manner of small temples, showing clear signs of neoclassical elements, which were soon used in other buildings. By 1860, the Cienfuegos Cathedral was the quintessential architectural model of the city. Murray's work gave a mark of identity to one of the most beautiful towns in Cuba.

The stained-glass on the façade was made in France and mounted in 1871. The glass in the round windows in the presbytery are from 1873, the same year in which the high altar was completed. The altar statue was carved in Barcelona. The church was consecrated as a cathedral on November 25, 1917. The organ was manufactured in Guipúzcoa and installed in 1920.

TEATRO TOMAS TERRY

TOMÁS TERRY THEATER

1887–1890

Lino Sánchez de Mármol, Engineer

This theater is an emblematic exponent of late nineteenth-century Cuban buildings of this kind. It was one of the first eclectic buildings built under the auspices of the Terry family, in honor of Don Tomás, founder of this lineage in Cienfuegos.

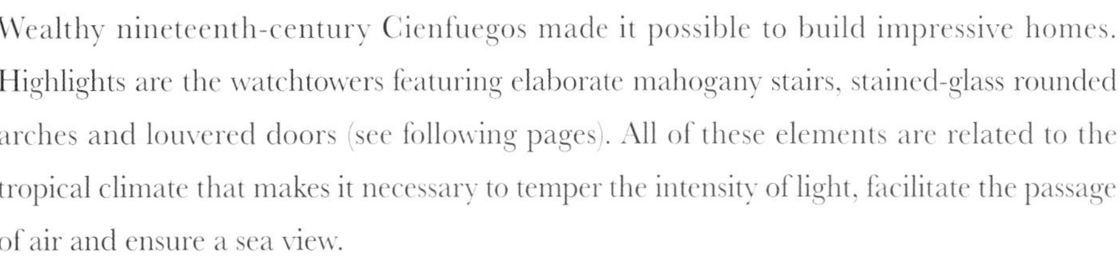

MANUEL BLANCO PALACE

1871–1878

Wealthy nineteenth-century Cienfuegos made it possible to build impressive homes. Highlights are the watchtowers featuring elaborate mahogany stairs, stained-glass rounded arches and louvered doors (see following pages). All of these elements are related to the tropical climate that makes it necessary to temper the intensity of light, facilitate the passage of air and ensure a sea view.

PASEO DEL PRADO

Notable nineteenth- and twentieth-century houses stand on both sides of Paseo del Prado. Urban requirements imposed the use of porches with supports made of wood or held by pillars and columns. The roofs, however, had to be flat. The construction of sloped roofs leaning toward the street was banned, thus giving the Cienfuegos Prado the grand architectural charm that distinguishes it. Statues, memorials, benches, streetlamps and other urban furnishings were placed in the center of the boulevard, adding to the merits and beauty of the site.

WOODEN HOUSES IN THE PUNTA GORDA PENINSULA

Frame houses built according to the new chalet-style homes that spread from the United States to the Caribbean from the mid-nineteenth century are still standing in Punta Gorda.

HOME OF PUYÍN

Late Nineteenth Century

Domingo Ferreiro, Master Builder

HOME OF CELESTINO CACES Y CARBONELL

Late Nineteenth Century

Casa de Visitas El Castillito

Domingo Ferreiro, Master Builder

TRINIDAD AND VALLE DE LOS INGENIOS

Trinidad was founded in early 1514 on the banks of the Arimao River (in today's Cienfuegos Province). The high concentration of indigenous population in Guamuhaya, however, was the deciding factor in relocating the town around the native village of Manzanilla—close to the Táyaba River, more or less in the center of the southern coast of Cuba—the seat of the *cacicazgo* (native American chiefdom headed by a *cacique*). For most of the sixteenth century, the native village and the Spanish town coexisted side by side until they melded into one single urban settlement.

Originally, it was a prosperous community thanks to the gold being panned on the shores of its rivers, but once the sources of the mineral ran dry, people started clearing out in an exodus toward other countries on the American continent. Abandoned by the Spanish, it was populated by surviving natives and the sons and daughters of Spaniards and Indian women—the first *criollos*, or Creole people. At the end of the sixteenth century, it would be resettled due to the fear that colonies might be set up inland by nations that were Spain's enemies.

The principal products of the area during its early centuries of existence were small fruits, cattle and tobacco. As for smuggling, this reached scandalous proportions encouraged by the relative isolation of the region and its proximity to the sea. In 1778, the port of Casilda was set up for trade with Spanish ports, and in 1792 the free introduction of slaves and machinery for the sugar mills was authorized. By the end of the century, the economic prosperity was being felt in a town considered to be the third in Cuba.

Keeping pace with economic progress, the old homes were remodeled and what became known as Trinidadian nineteenth-century architecture took hold. An incredible wave of construction was taking place. The city grew from north to south, from east to west. The lower town areas, closest to the coast, were urbanized along the classical grid system and based on the new urban focal points—Carrillo Square, Isabel II Square and Campo de Marte. The city's populated area doubled. Paving the streets began in 1827 and had been almost completed by mid-century when sidewalk paving was also begun. In the midst of this splendor, however, the signs of ruin were already present.

The economic breakup of Trinidad had many causes, but the principal one was its dependence on sugar. By 1840, when all the land in the San Luis Valley had been occupied, capital and people began to emigrate to other regions such as Sancti Spíritus, Sagua la Grande and, especially, to Cienfuegos in order to expand new economic enterprises.

The appearance of beet sugar, whose industrialized process could be done at a lower cost, resulted in unequal competition between Cuban and European sugar producers. The Cuban land barons were forced to make a decision: either industrialize or maintain their by now obsolete slave-owner status. Some residents of Trinidad, such as Justo Germán Cantero, improved the technology of his factories. In 1843, Cantero installed the Derosne train on his Güinía de Soto Sugar Mill, which was one of the principal mills in the valley, but most of the production units existing in the area were working with Jamaican or French trains or consisted of simple *trapiches* moved by animal power. Finding it impossible to convert to new technologies because this involved far too much of an investment, Trinidad's land barons opted to hold on to slavery.

But slavery led them straight into a blind alley. The high cost of keeping slaves along with the difficulties involved in their purchase forced them to stop producing white sugar and become producers of what was called concentrated sugar, that is, muscovado. Even so, costs skyrocketed. Year after year, the land barons' debts piled up and they submitted to Spanish and foreign traders who, in the absence of banks, played the roles of financers and ended up taking economic control of the valley's sugar production. The industry went bankrupt and trade came to a standstill.

The secular town remained frozen in time, with its cobbled streets, its large old houses, its atmosphere of unchanged past. This gives the city an extraordinary heritage value. In 1988, Trinidad and the Valle de los Ingenios were listed by UNESCO as a World Heritage Site.

PLAZA MAYOR

An expanded and complex layout, this is not the square where the city was founded. This area was developed at the end of the seventeenth century as portico for the main parish church. The Plaza Mayor took on its final configuration when the early church was demolished, a new one was built in its place, and the houses surrounding it were remodeled or built during the nineteenth century. Street paving started in 1827.

On September 19, 1856, a recreational park started to be built. It was completed in 1857 according to the project of engineer Julio Sagebien Delgado, with the assistance of Julio Bastida Tardío of Trinidad and under the auspices of Governor Luis M. Serrano. In 1868, public cisterns were built in order to take advantage of the differences of levels with Cristo Street. At first, the railings had oil-burning lampposts. In honor of the visit of Antonia Domínguez de Guevara Borrell and her husband Captain General Francisco Serrano, gas lighting was installed in 1859 along with free-standing lampposts. The plaza mayor and its architectural milieu make up Cuba's best conserved and most coherent colonial urban complex.

HOME OF THE SÁNCHEZ IZNAGA SISTERS

Eighteenth/Nineteenth Centuries
Museo de Arquitectura

This lovely, significant large house is the result of bringing together two homes. The first one was a masonry and tile lean-to with its façade facing a small square called Plazoleta de la Sacristía. Around 1750, this building became part of the newly laid-out residence whose façade was turned towards Plaza Mayor. Its beautiful ceilings date approximately to that time. A porch was added in 1789. It is quite probable that a neighboring house was built that same year to serve as slave quarters. In 1819, María del Carmen Borrell Padrón bought both buildings and in 1886 her granddaughter Concepción Iznaga del Valle, wife of Saturnino Sánchez, inherited them. Around that date they were brought together and remodeled to acquire the appearance they have today.

JOSÉ RAFAEL ORTIZ PALACE

1809

Galería de Artes Plásticas

In 1809, Town Councilor José Rafael Ortiz built this beautiful mansion. Without heirs, his will read that at his death (occurring in 1834) and that of his wife (occurring in 1857), the house was to pass "to poor beggars so that they would benefit from its leasing." When the children's home was created, rent from the house went to support that institution and subsequently, the General Wood Hospital. In 1920, Saturnino Sánchez bought it at an auction held by the hospital.

The house stands out for its lovely wooden balcony featuring a small tiled roof; but its most striking feature are the conserved murals painted in the spirit of the rococo and the style of Louis XVI.

45 REAL DEL JIGÜE STREET

1750

Restaurante Sol Ananda

This is an old dwelling that conserves the low ceiling of the early houses, the original roofs and the building techniques of the walls.

CONDE BRUNET PALACE

1830

Museo Romántico

The Conde Brunet Palace is one of the most eye-catching buildings of the complex. It was built in the nineteenth century to replace an ancient building that had been bought by José Mariano Borrell Padrón in 1802. In 1830, the residence went to Borrell's daughter Ángela and it was reconstructed for her wedding to Nicolás Brunet Muñoz that same year. The façade is outstanding for its novel feature of a porch with arches supported by brick pillars, similar to those that were being added in those same years to residences at the sugar mills in the San Luis Valley. Also worth mentioning is the balcony covered by eaves with cyma moldings and crowned by parapets with goblet-shaped caps in the picturesque manner that these elements were used in Trinidad.

Several elements make their appearance for the first time in the interiors: pantries protected by radiating shutters; openings that are closed with lacquered mahogany doors, decorated with striated wooden pilasters and corner medallions highlighted with gold leaf; and shutter screens protecting the exterior openings. The rooms surround the inner courtyard on three of its sides, joined to each other by balcony-corridors held up by braces; the kitchen stands out for its fireplace and bell canopy (see following pages).

In the twentieth century, the building was purchased by Antonio Frías who sold it on January 10, 1947, to the Asociación Pro-Trinidad to become a museum. On April 21, 1959, it became property of the Cuban State.

SANTÍSIMA TRINIDAD MAIN PARISH CHURCH

1892

Emilio Echeverría, Master Builder

In 1664, work on a new church was begun on the lot where the parish church stands today. Completed in 1692, the church was demolished in 1817 when the long process of building the Santísima Trinidad began. Its final building phase started in 1867. It was consecrated on February 15, 1892, by Bishop Manuel Santander after 75 years of construction at a cost of over 100,000 pesos. The towers, however, were still incomplete.

Santísima Trinidad is one of the largest churches in Cuba. It has a remarkable false vault made of wooden trusses coated with plaster over the principal nave. This is a truly majestic structure surpassing the scale of its square. Its interior has some outstanding images from the original older main parish church, from the San Francisco Church and from donations by Trinidadian families. In the early twentieth century, Father Amadeo Fiogere designed and worked personally on the lovely neo-Gothic altars made with precious Cuban wood, placed on the at the high altar and in the side chapels (see following pages).

The Christ of Veracruz is a figure that has been venerated by generations of Trinidadians. It was acquired in 1714 by Nicolás Pablo Vélez and then donated to the city's main church.

JUSTO GERMÁN CANTERO PALACE

1829

Museo de Historia Municipal

It is one of the most remarkable homes in Cuba, built from 1827 to 1829, possibly by the Scottish architect Vitruvio Steegers (principal architect/builder in Trinidad in 1828) for José Mariano Borrell Padrón. When Borrell Padrón died in 1830, the home went to his son and heir José Mariano Borrell Lemus. In 1841, Borrell Lemus sold it to his cousin Monserrate de Lara, widow of Iznaga, who shortly after married Justo Germán Cantero. With a very tall ceiling—seven meters at the ridgepole—this mansion was the model of the by-now classical layout of local domestic architecture. Decorated by Italian artist Daniel Dall'Aglio, its rooms are outstanding for their extravagance, while the elegant tower reaffirms the prestige of this exceptional building.

The Pro-Trinidad Association acquired it in 1947, making it the first school of arts and trades in Trinidad. In 1975, restoration was begun on the murals. The museum was inaugurated in 1981.

406 GUTIÉRREZ STREET

1830/1930

Hostal Casa de Lara

This house was bought by José González Llorente some time between 1828 and 1831. In 1865, his son, Antonio González Llorente, sold it to Ramón Soto del Valle who enlarged it by increasing its depth. The layout featured two areas in front of the house consisting of *aposentos and recámaras* to one side; the dining room in the galleries; the bedroom and backyard in the rear. Soto del Valle built a great cistern in the backyard and kept the kitchen with its hearth and chimney. He also bought a plot of land from Monserrate de Lara at the back which fronted onto Gloria Street, the site of Candamo, the city's first theater, destroyed in the hurricane of 1837. After the death of Soto del Valle in 1879, the house went to his daughter Rosa, who remarried Felipe de Lara Hernández.

For many years this was the residence of the prestigious Trinidadian physician, Dr. Luis Felipe de Lara Soto del Valle (1894–1984). In 1936, Dr. Lara enlarged his residence when he built a second home on the back lot. The new construction followed plans drawn up by engineer Hugo Bastida. The layout revolved around a courtyard and was in continuance with the original building. It followed neo-colonial principles in strict adherence with the era's municipal bylaws, which prohibited anything that did not harmonize with the old colonial structures. The result was a remarkable complex showing the evolution of local architecture within the span of one century. Because of its excellent state of typological conservation, it is one of the most authentic examples of homes in the city.

ARCHEOLOGICAL SITE AT THE SAN ISIDRO DE LOS DESTILADEROS SUGAR MILL

First Half of the Nineteenth Century

The early nineteenth century saw the introduction of modern technology as well as the so-called Jamaican or French train for heating sugar at Trinidad's sugar mills. The train at the San Isidro Mill is, so far, the only one that has been excavated in Cuba.

The mill's *batey* was a small village consisting of a main house, the sugar workers' homes, the slave quarters, industrial buildings, supporting production facilities, aqueduct and installations for conveying water, and the tower.

Above and Right:

COUNTRY HOUSE AT THE GUÁIMARO SUGAR MILL

Late Eighteenth Century/First Decades of the Nineteenth Century

Owned by José Mariano Borrell y Padrón, the Guáimaro sugar mill produced 82,000 *arrobas* of muscovado and purged sugar, becoming the world's top producer in 1827. Borrell then built what came to be called the Cantero Palace and modernized the mill's dwelling house, one of the most beautiful of its kind.

Opposite Page:

THE MANACA-IZNAGA SUGAR MILL TOWER

The striking Manaca-Iznaga Tower was built by Alejo Iznaga y Borrell in 1828. This architectural wonder could also be attributed to the architect Vitruvio Steegers.

CANTERO.

SANCTI SPÍRITUS

In the center of Cuba, at a distance from the coastline, Sancti Spíritus grew with unstable prosperity. Its location inland isolated it from the rest of the country and from the Spanish Caribbean territories. Locked up in itself, its growth was irregular. This may explain how its architecture developed by reusing available structures, which resulted in the complex constructive stratification noticeable in its buildings. It was customary in this town to build the new on top of the old and so a rich profile of superimposed eras turns it into the most "medieval" of our early towns.

The extremely twisting layout of the streets abounds in narrow and curving alleys, like nearly hidden paths within the complex labyrinth of roads that draw near the Jesús Nazareno neighborhood. Small triangular "squares" are formed at the intersections, where arterial streets converge. This gives rise to a picturesque urban scene that may be confusing to those who are unfamiliar with the city, but also exciting to anyone who enjoys travelling through the past.

MAIN PARISH CHURCH

1612–1692/1764

The main parish church of Sancti Spíritus is considered the best conserved of all the churches erected during the seventeenth century. As was customary in early centuries, the church stands to the side of the square. The collar-beam roof and the presbytery's octagonal roof were built in 1666. This church exhibits the only preserved wooden toral arch, a piece of extraordinary value that documents the antiquity of this monument. The church has two separate chapels built unto the principal nave: Humility and Patience, a cult that was practiced in the country since the seventeenth century, and the Rosario funeral chapel, property of the influential Pérez de Corcha family from Sancti Spíritus.

The tall tower was completed in the mid-eighteenth century and marks the center point of the half-league circle that establishes the limits of the town's common land.

3 MÁXIMO GÓMEZ STREET

1740–Nineteenth Century

Museo de Historia

Former dwelling and clear example of the superimposition of structures from different eras. The wooden ceilings (not shown) are part of the original structure; the façade was modified during the first half of the nineteenth century with the inclusion of eaves with cyma moldings and iron railings with ogee canopies. A second open arched-roof gallery was added during the second half of the seventeenth century.

VALLE PALACE

1759/1846/1862

Museo de Arte Colonial

Object to successive expansions, this structure, also known as the House of the One Hundred Doors, excels both for its architecture and its valuable collection of vintage objects—originally owned by the Valle family—displayed in the rooms. Its graceful façade and interior elements such as wood and glass screen doors, and stained-glass rounded arches date back to the remodeling performed in 1862.

CÉSPEDES (AT THE CORNER OF VALDIVIA)

Ca. 1860

Wall decorations on the façade that extend to the eaves are typical of houses in Sancti Spíritus.

YAYABO BRIDGE

1831

Domingo Valverde and Blas Cabrera, Master Builders

Symbol of the city par excellence, this bridge is still in use despite its considerable age.

SANTA CLARA

Santa Clara became prominent in the late nineteenth century and the early twentieth century. Centrally located, Vidal Park is surrounded by the town's most important buildings.

HOME OF CLARA CARTA PONS

Ca. 1834

Museo de Artes Decorativas

This residence is one of the few from the colonial period that has survived without major changes. It is built around a spacious courtyard surrounded by galleries held up by wooden posts. Its rooms contain valuable objects and furniture from the nineteenth century.

1884
TEATRO LA CARIDAD.
1885
ERIGIDO POR Dª MARTA ABREU DE ESTEVEZ
PARA SOCORRER EN MEMORIA DE SUS PADRES,
A LOS POBRES DE SANTA CLARA

LA CARIDAD THEATER

1885

La Caridad Theater is also one of the largest Cuban arenas. Sponsored by philanthropist Marta Abreu de Estévez, it still exhibits the original architectural structure, ambience and decorations. The latter were made by the renowned Filipino artist Camilo Salaya.

REMEDIOS

Remedios was formally established by the famous Spanish conquistador Vasco Porcallo de Figueroa (ca. 1492–1550) on the north-central Cuban coast to serve as support for the expeditions to conquer Mexico and Florida.

A place of intense sea traffic and a safe haven for ships plying the Old Bahamas Channel, the people of Remedios devoted themselves to trade, both legal and illegal. Its fame for being a rich place turned out to be a magnet for the pirate attacks occurring on country estates and the town. The pillaging terrified the residents who requested that the town be relocated further inland. With the terror behind them and not being able to come to an agreement, a terrible dispute ensued, which caused the town to be set on fire and destroyed in 1691. In spite of this, Remedios emerged from the ashes and by the mid-nineteenth century had attained a position of notable relevance.

SAN JUAN BAUTISTA MAIN PARISH CHURCH

Ca. 1578/1610/1735–1757

Like other religious buildings of Cuba's early towns, San Juan Bautista de Remedios Church is a Mudéjar-Renaissance church with the most splendidly conserved collar-beam roof in the country, second to none of its kind in Spanish America. The church was refurbished and expanded between 1735 and 1757 with the addition of the current presbytery. The height of the ceiling was raised and the façade modified. Its original version was similar to sixteenth-century Mexican churches.

The collar-beam framework differs from others of its kind in Cuba in its decoration, which covers almost all of the framework, and uses the typical plant motifs of Mudéjar inspiration and scenes of everyday life, as a remarkable testimony of an era and sense of belonging to a given place. The tie beams, angle braces, beam hangers and fascia boards have volute geometric patterns, painted with black dye on the reddish wooden background. The planking is enhanced with four-petal roses, painted in a single flat color. Black was used to outline the image, and white, blue, yellow and red were used to fill in the image. The roses are framed in continuous trails of foliage, of Renaissance themes painted in black.

The altars of this church are considered the most complete of their kind in Cuba. They were placed during the restoration of the church from 1944 to 1954 under the auspices of benefactor Eutimio Falla Bonet; the design was by the architect Aquiles Maza and the advisory by the archaeologist Francisco Prat Puig.

51 ANTONIO MACEO STREET

1850

This house is an excellent example of the introduction of a new type of dwelling in Remedios during the mid-nineteenth century. A door situated on the side of the structure gives access to the house through a *zaguán*. The small parlor is decorated with rounded arches fitted with stained-glass panes. These elements were greatly developed in the mid-nineteenth century. In addition to the original elements and distribution of the house, it still conserves the furniture and ambience of the nineteenth century, which makes it a remarkable national exponent.

114 MAXÍMO GÓMEZ STREET

1860

Hotel Mascotte

During the mid-nineteenth century, the scale of the city, which mainly consisted of one-story structures, was broken by the construction of airy, two-story, academic-style buildings, with the typical pilasters, cornices, canopies, corbels and other elements related to neoclassicism.

This house was used as residence of the Spanish lieutenant governors. At the end of the first Independence War in 1878, it was transformed into a hotel. In 1898, Major General Máximo Gomez and Mr. Robert P. Porter, commissioner of U.S. President William McKinley, met here to agree the terms for demobilizing the Cuban Liberation Army.

CAMAGÜEY

Initially set up on the shores of today's Nuevitas Bay, Camagüey Province—previously known as Santa María del Puerto Príncipe—the town was moved in 1516 to a site in the province's interior. In 1528, it was definitively relocated to the center of the province between the Tínima and Jatibonico rivers, equally distant from either coast. Its flatlands became pastures for large herds of cattle whose meat and skins constituted the primary source of its economic growth. The 1778 census has it as the second largest city in Cuba. Its characteristic features, therefore, took shape between the end of the eighteenth century and the beginning of the nineteenth century, and it tended to resist changes in the years that followed, thereby giving this colonial complex a distinctive air.

The city plan has an irregular layout in the form of a "cracked plate," a comparison alluding to its circular perimeter and the serpentine nature of its streets interrupted by numerous small squares. This urban configuration, however, was the result of history rather than a conscious intention. At first, the city was laid out on a regular plan but the need for defense from pirate attacks made it advisable to break up the linear nature of the streets in order to confuse the attacking enemy.

Because of its urban and architectural merit, a section of the historical center was declared a UNESCO World Heritage Site on July 8, 2008.

SAN JUAN DE DIOS SQUARE

San Juan de Dios Square is a well-preserved colonial complex that still maintains the urban layout and the buildings erected in the eighteenth and nineteenth centuries.

SAN JUAN DE DIOS CHURCH AND HOSPITAL

1736/1756–1848

This church is one of the oldest in the city. It still preserves its original interior layout, the wooden ceilings and the doors. The facade was remodeled in the nineteenth century, as was the neighboring hospital. The body of Major General Ignacio Agramonte y Loynaz (1841–1873), one of the most beloved figures in Cuban history, was laid to rest in the cloister gallery, which has made this a place of permanent veneration.

There is no greater testimony to the extraordinary splendor of Camagüey than its churches and convents; religious structures that spread the Spanish-Mudéjar, baroque, neoclassical and eclectic architectural styles.

NUESTRA SEÑORA DE LA MERCED CHURCH AND CONVENT

Ca. 1730

La Merced is an amazing edifice, considered a work of considerable caliber for the country and the era, inspired by the architectural principles disseminated by Sebastiano Serlio. The church contains valuable paintings and images, especially the Holy Sepulcher, crafted in silver by Mexican silversmith Juan Benítez Alfonso in 1762.

NUESTRA SEÑORA DEL CARMEN CHURCH

1823–1825

Cristóbal Troyano, Architect

This church was built next to the women's hospital, under the auspices of renowned Father Valencia. Its construction is similar to other works promoted by this priest, such as the San Lázaro Hospital (1819). Father Valencia's works were carried out by the Andalusian master builder Cristóbal Troyano (1762–1822). A combination of Spanish-Elizabethan Gothic, mixtilineal and ogee arches were incorporated in these versions of the late baroque period.

URSULINE CONVENT

1826–1829/1909

Oficina del

Historiador de la Ciudad

The Ursuline Convent was built next to the Del Carmen Church in 1829 for young girls from Camaguey. It was rebuilt from 1908 to 1909.

459 IGNACIO AGRAMONTE STREET

Ca. 1800–1810

Museo Casa Natal de Ignacio Agramonte y Loynaz

Backed by a solid economic development, the splendid residences of Camaguey's gentry are one of the best expressions of Cuban colonial architecture. This was rightly acknowledged by Robert T. Hill in his book *Cuba and Porto Rico with other Islands of the West Indies*, published in 1898. He said that Camaguey was "the chief interior city of Cuba, and claims to be the most Creole of Cuban towns."

The house of the Agramonte family is one of the few in the provinces to have a mezzanine. The courtyard still exhibits *tinajones*, large earthenware jars for collecting rainwater, situated one behind the other, as was customary in the city.

AMALIA SIMONI VILLA

1848

Casa de la Mujer Camagüeyana

This summerhouse was built by José Ramón Simoni Ricardo, father of Amalia, wife of Ignacio Agramonte. Remodeled in the second half of the nineteenth century, two elements were incorporated: a neo-classical portico enclosed by doors and rounded arches with fan-shaped shutters, and a room on the top floor whose role was that of a lookout. The house has large courtyards surrounded by galleries and beautiful gardens.

CHORRO DE MAÍTA ARCHAEOLOGICAL SITE, BANES

Located in Banes, Holguín Province, in an area that used to be part of Bayamo, the Chorro de Maíta Archaeological Site is one of the areas considered to have been occupied for the longest period of time—from the tenth to the sixteenth centuries. It is also the most important evidence of Indo-Hispanic coexistence discovered in Cuba to date. In the cemetery, a total of 108 skeletons were dug out in an area of 2,000 square meters, part of a large settlement where an aboriginal village has been replicated.

According to archaeologist Jesús M. Guarch Delmonte, who directed the excavation works and the replication of the site-based museum, Banes was, for a long time, "a province of Indians," a reservoir of indigenous people who continued to live like before the Spanish conquest until the arrival of Spaniards in the area in the mid-sixteenth century.

GIBARA

Gibara was founded in 1817 as the port for the city of Holguín. In a few years, it became the most prosperous trading enclave on Cuba's northeastern coast. From the mid-nineteenth century, lovely residences were built that were distinguished by the whiteness of their walls. For this reason, Gibara came to be called The White City. New technologies arrived by sea from the United States of America. Among the city's many architectural novelties, the most outstanding are creative interpretations in wood on the neoclassical theme.

PLAZA MAYOR

The original urban center of Gibara (not shown) is very small and its layout is not strictly orthogonal. The main buildings are situated in the vicinity of this square, located in the historical center.

SAN FULGENCIO CHURCH
1850–1853
Juan Pons, Architect

Of true neoclassical lineage, the church stands out for the serene composition of its parts, with the main nave guarded by solidly built towers on both sides.

CASINO ESPAÑOL

1885

Museo de Ciencias Naturales

This tall edifice has a large portal with rounded columns that support a simulated entablature crowned with cornice and parapet. The interior stands out for the transparency created by the arches between the front rooms and the arches surrounding the courtyard, which is protected by beautiful stained-glass rounded arches.

HOME OF
MARCELINO GARRIDO

Second Half of the Nineteenth Century
Casa de Cultura

This is a superb house built around a spacious courtyard surrounded by galleries. Inside, the stained-glass rounded arches and wooden screens stand out.

MANUEL DA SILVA HOUSE

1888/1889

According to records, the house built by José Romero on this plot of land in 1781 was the first in the city. On the same plot, Da Silva erected four large houses with courtyards in the late nineteenth century. All four houses share a large porch and are considered some of Gibara's most typical houses.

BAYAMO

Bayamo lies on the side of the river of the same name, a tributary of the Cauto River, on the bank that opens up in the shape of a fault serving as boundary to the flat expanse of land where the city was settled. Founded in 1513, it was the second town created by Diego Velázquez. During the First War of Independence (1868–1878), it was captured by the troops of Carlos Manuel de Céspedes, the Father of the Nation. It was in Bayamo that the Cuban National Anthem was first sung. Cuban rebels were unable to hold back the Spanish onslaught so the town's people burned down the city in 1869 as the rebels retreated. It is a much venerated place where you can still hear the crackle of flames in the air and sense the marks left by the heroic immolation.

Its urban layout, though, is living proof of the forms adopted by Caribbean cities prior to the conquest and reformulation of Mexico City in 1523. The Spanish town was situated at the center, configured by two streets that intersected each other perpendicularly, much like the city-encampments of the Late Middle Ages in Spain, and made up of parallel streets that tended to be regular. To the sides of that center were the neighborhoods reserved for the natives: Caneyes Arriba and Caneyes Abajo, identifiable by their peculiar irregular layout.

173

SAN SALVADOR MAIN PARISH CHURCH

1609–1613/Twentieth Century

Plaza del Himno Nacional

Located near the town center, the original cathedral was destroyed by an earthquake in 1551. The new church was erected on the Bayamo River, near the San Francisco Convent, which was founded in 1582. The irregular layout of the area is the result of the rapid and uncontrolled growth of the town in the late sixteenth and early seventeenth centuries, when it reached a population of over 1,500 inhabitants, a huge number at the time. The parish church was built with thick brick walls, and despite the many transformations undertaken throughout the years, its structure remains essentially the same as when it was first built under the influence of traditional Spanish constructions of the late Middle Ages. Divided into one or three naves with wooden framework roofs, its structure stands out for the triangular arrangement of the main façade. The church was rebuilt in the early nineteenth century with the addition of a one-story portico with a stained-glass rounded arch in the center and two arched openings on either side. This portico was one of Cuba's first neoclassical structures. The church was remodeled again in 1919 with the addition of a second story over the nineteenth-century portico. The bell tower was made taller.

NUESTRA SEÑORA DE LOS DOLORES CHAPEL

1738–1740

Built to one side of the main parish church, this is considered one of Cuba's most beautiful religious buildings and a testament to the town's early opulence. It is also one of the few monuments that survived the fire. Topped with pinnacles covered with Delftware tiles, the center of its triangular façade is crowned with an oculus for interior lighting—a common solution used in Renaissance constructions.

According to Francisco Prat Puig, the framework with corbels inserted in the tie beams is probably an imitation of the one originally found in the main parish church. The *harneruelo* (central part of a ceiling) has been profusely decorated with painted carved wooden elements, featuring splendid double corbels that end in Plateresque-inspired scrolls, as is common in eastern Cuba. The baroque altarpiece is an exquisite piece, with carvings depicting local fruits as an expression of the Creole identity.

NUESTRA SEÑORA DE LA LUZ CHURCH

Seventeenth Century/Twentieth Century

Sala-teatro José Joaquín Palma

Destroyed by the fire, the old church gained in importance thanks to the restoration works directed by Cuban-American architect Walter Betancourt (1932–1978), who was based in Santiago de Cuba and from whom we inherited a perfect example of creative reconciliation between old and new elements. The respect he felt for the historic dimension of the monument did not limit Betancourt from highlighting the expressive potential of both traditional and modern construction materials in reconciliation with the strength of the volumes and the studied effects of light on surfaces and colors. This is a work of elevated design complemented by its detailed execution.

57 ANTONIO MACEO STREET

Nineteenth Century
Museo Casa Natal de
Carlos Manuel de Céspedes

Originally a one-story dwelling, this house was expanded to two stories and remodeled in 1833, according to the date inscribed on the balcony railing. Destroyed by the fire, it was rebuilt either in the late nineteenth or the early twentieth century. The house was restored by Francisco Prat Puig, who showed great respect for the enormous architectural and historical significance of the building. The museum treasures valuable pieces related to the lives of Céspedes and other patriots from the city of Bayamo.

SANTIAGO DE CUBA

Santiago de Cuba was founded on high ground, to the side and at the rear of an immense bay surrounded by mountains. The city is distinguished by its striking urban views, for its attachment to the Spanish-Mudéjar building traditions and for the incorporation of formal solutions in the nineteenth and twentieth centuries that had arrived from the Caribbean. The blending of such diverse components resulted in its lovely and distinctive personality.

Santiago de Cuba was the place from where Diego Velázquez, the Spanish Crown's representative in the New World, organized voyages to explore the Gulf of Mexico. This is well-known history, which eventually led his relative—and later enemy—Hernán Cortés to conquer the spectacular Aztec Empire. The conquest of Mexico signified the decline of Velázquez's prominence and with it that of Santiago de Cuba, which was superseded by Havana, whose port soon became acknowledged to be the most suitable place to reach the Gulf Stream. Discovered by the mariner Antón de Alaminos, the Gulf Stream facilitated the return of ships to Spain. Since then, one of the features of the collective idiosyncrasy of Santiago is the contrast between East and West in Cuba.

In 1662, an English attack destroyed the city, but after that event productive trade relations were established with England and, through them, with the Western Caribbean. The Treaty of Utrecht of 1713 gave England the monopoly of the slave trade and one of the two factories that were built in Cuba by virtue of that treaty was established in Santiago de Cuba. At the end of the eighteenth century and the beginning of the nineteenth century, Franco-Haitian immigrants fleeing the ravages of the Revolution in Saint Domingue brought economic and cultural renewal with them to the region.

But in the end, the balance of economic development would be tipped in favor of the western part of Cuba. The weakness of local capital was undoubtedly the cause of the unique physiognomy of Santiago de Cuba given that the houses of the upper class did not go beyond what had been established by Creole tradition, and the homes of the middle and working classes maintained many of the ancient construction practices. Some unimaginable "reconciliations" appeared in Santiago de Cuba: column studs finished with "Ionic-Mudéjar" bases, overhanging eaves crowned with cornices, "baroque" doorways and cornices, neoclassical doorways with overhanging tops… In Santiago de Cuba time lost its historical sequencing, and processes, which elsewhere followed a logical course, all occurred at the same time.

Should this be all there is, then Santiago de Cuba's architecture would be a very special case. But there's more. Triumphal arches became widespread, as well as wooden ceilings, wooden shutters enclosing balconies, plain or embossed tin parapets, dormers, plastered wood-strip walls nailed side by side to the supporting posts and wood openwork pedestals. Such elements are typical of wooden Caribbean houses, which is consistent with the well-defined local Spanish-Creole tradition resulting in the singular appearance that characterizes the architecture of Santiago de Cuba.

At present, Santiago de Cuba is the second largest city in Cuba and it holds priceless tangible and intangible heritage treasures. The Castillo de San Pedro de la Roca del Morro was declared a World Heritage Site by UNESCO in 1997; in 2000, the Archeological Landscape of the First Coffee Plantations in the South-East of Cuba was also listed as a World Heritage Site; and in 2003, the tumba francesa Caridad de Oriente was declared Masterpiece of the Oral and Intangible Heritage of Humanity.

PLAZA MAYOR/CARLOS MANUEL DE CÉSPEDES PARK

Santiago de Cuba's Plaza Mayor is one of the oldest squares in the Americas. It is surrounded by buildings that are greatly appreciated for their historical and cultural impact. It was initially designed following an orthogonal plan inspired by the grid model. In the mid-seventeenth century, engineer Juan de Císcara adjusted the layout of the city. The center was occupied by the Plaza Mayor, site of the *cabildo* and parish church from the days of the city's foundation.

Plaza Mayor: firstly, Céspedes Park; the City Hall to the right; the Diego Velázquez Fort/Residence in the foreground; and the bay and mountains in the background

DIEGO VELÁZQUEZ FORT/RESIDENCE

Ca. 1520–Late Eighteenth Century

Museo de Ambiente Histórico Cubano

On one side of Plaza Mayor, on today's Félix Pena (Santo Tomás) and Aguilera (Marina) streets, stands the oldest building in Cuba and one of the first to be built in the West Indies. This really was not a dwelling per se, but a two-story fort built of stone, with a single bay placed parallel to Marina Street. On this side, we can see the original entranceway with its corresponding praetorium, which, although it is mutilated, is the first to have overcome the difficult slopes of Santiago's hilly topography.

In the late eighteenth century, the building grew along Santo Tomás Street and turned its façade toward the square, transforming its military aspect into a residential one, thereby giving the monument its current appearance after its restoration by Francisco Prat Puig in the 1970s. Prat Puig left evidence of the enlargements to the original building visible. Besides keeping the original entranceway on Marina Street, the partial closure of the courtyard window can be seen as the result of building an arched gallery that today runs parallel to Santo Tomás St. Prat also kept visible the uprights built into the gallery walls and elsewhere in the structure. All this suggests that the building underwent two remodeling episodes: the first one done in a traditional manner and bringing with it the new orientation of the façade toward the square, and the second one assimilating the wooden structures within the galleries built on arches held up by pillars, thereby giving the building a neoclassical appearance.

METROPOLITAN BASILICA CATHEDRAL

1528–1555/1666–1670/1766/
1852/1916–1922/1932

In spite of its many transformations, the Cathedral of Santiago de Cuba is the oldest church in Cuba. It started to be built on the south side of Plaza Mayor in 1528 and was made of stone, with a tile roof. The new church was begun around 1679 and completed in 1690. It was rebuilt in 1810 and the façade was oriented toward the square.

The church as we see it today was built over the earlier ones by Santiago architect Carlos Segrera. It has conserved valuable objects, paintings and furnishings, such as the *Ecce Homo*, believed to be the oldest painting in Cuba; the *Coro de los Canónigos* (Canon Choir), extraordinary example of the carpenter's art; the ceiling paintings made by Dominican painter Luis Desangles in 1922; and numerous religious objects that are kept in the Archdiocese Museum adjacent to the cathedral. Seriously damaged by Hurricane Sandy in 2012, it was restored for the 500th anniversary of the city's founding.

SAN BASILIO EL MAGNO SEMINARY

1774

Centro Cultural Francisco Prat Puig

Two houses were bought in 1774 to install the San Basilio el Magno Seminary, one of the country's oldest higher education centers, founded in 1722. The two houses were joined into one building, whose courtyard is outstanding for its spacious two-story gallery held up by wooden posts and protected by wooden balustrades. The roof is supported by wooden posts that are embedded in the walls, testimony to the ancient, deep-rooted traditional building techniques.

SANTO TOMÁS SQUARE

SANTO TOMÁS CHURCH

1715–1720

Santo Tomás Church, which is also on the side of its square, follows the basic layout of Mudéjar churches defined since the Late Middle Ages in Spain: rectangular floor plan with one or three naves, collar-beam roof and a tower on one side.

352 FÉLIX PENA STREET

Late Eighteenth Century

From the mid-eighteenth century, a new element was incorporated into the façades: the corridor, a sort of balcony accessible from the street. It was originally called *altozano*, hillock in English, and prohibited for a long time by the local *cabildo* until the city's growth above its height made this solution a necessity.

GENERAL PORTUONDO (AT THE CORNER OF CALLEJÓN)

One-story houses predominated due to the fear of earthquakes. Those having loftier status used roofs with tie beams and tracery, but the most common roofs in Santiago de Cuba were made of *rollizos*, rounded unfinished pieces of timber. These appeared mostly in lean-to houses. Lean-to roofs are very simple with a single slope that starts at the façade and gradually descends to the back of the house.

Lean-to houses perpetuate a popular typology coming from remote origins when the presence of praetoriums or small staircases imbedded on the outside walls was almost constant to make up for the difference of levels between the houses and the streets. They predominated in the seventeenth century all over the country. Santiago de Cuba examples date back to the eighteenth and nineteenth centuries.

260 HEREDIA STREET

Early Nineteenth Century

Museo Casa Natal de José M. Heredia

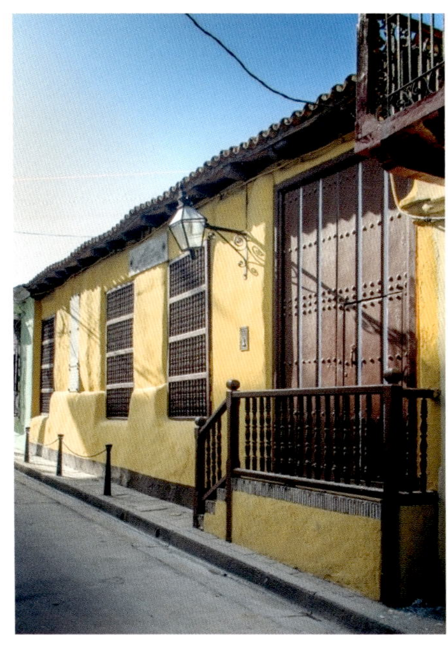

Santiago de Cuba homes have either one or two stories and in general are made of long, flexible poles called *cuje*, a construction material that does not allow any architectural additions, which explains the smooth walls lacking any ornamentation. *Cuje* is a construction system made up of posts embedded in the walls to support the roofs. The spaces between the posts are filled with cross poles and crushed rock mixed with lime. In the event of an earth tremor, the softer parts will fall but the wooden supports are able to move and therefore stay standing. The lightness of the buildings was also emphasized by the use of wooden dividing walls, like a partition, to isolate one space from another. In the late eighteenth century or early nineteenth century, the wooden dividers located between the parlor and the small parlor. or between the parlor and the gallery were frequently highlighted with lobed arches.

266 HEREDIA STREET

Ca. 1830

Sede Provincial de la Unión de Escritores y Artistas de Cuba (UNEAC)

In Cuban colonial houses, the courtyard was the heart of the household. Galleries represented the transition from the open space under the sky to the rooms. These galleries served as shields from the rain and glaring sun, and passageways for the breeze to blow. The life of the family revolved around the gallery. The parapet of the wells presided over the courtyard, whether modest or sumptuous, made of marble or masonry. This completes the image of the traditional courtyard. Santiago de Cuba's Morro is a spectacular edifice perching on the cliff that serves as its base, cut through by impressive stairways. It is a powerful and beautiful monument whose silhouette is part of the wonderful natural scenery that provides a magnificent backdrop.

SAN PEDRO DE LA ROCA OR MORRO CASTLE

1639–Eighteenth Century

Museo Histórico

Juan Bautista Antonelli, Engineer

The construction of the fortress of Santiago de Cuba was commissioned to military engineer Juan Bautista Antonelli during the government of Pedro de la Roca y Borja (1633–1643). The project consisted of a castle situated on a high rock overlooking the entrance to the channel of the bay. El Morro was actually built during the tenure of Pedro de Bayona Villanueva (1654–1659) and destroyed during the assault of the English in 1662. Juan de Císcara later drafted the project for its reconstruction. The lower platform was completed in 1674. The castle's current walls, as well as the moat, ravalin and outer parapet situated on the eastern façade were built from 1690 to 1693. Additions were made to the structure during the eighteenth and nineteenth centuries.

Santiago de Cuba's Morro is a spectacular edifice perching on the cliff that serves as its base, cut through by impressive stairways. It is a powerful and beautiful monument whose silhouette is part of the wonderful natural scenery that provides a magnificent backdrop.

BARACOA

Located at the north-easternmost tip of Cuba, Baracoa is a beautiful place, but rather difficult to reach. Its proximity to Hispaniola, the concentration of native population, its fertile soil and splendid rain forest vegetation favored the settlement of a town on the banks of large rivers, under the shadow of a lofty crag and overlooking a lovely bay. Nevertheless, this first one of Cuba's towns was temporarily abandoned as it was almost inaccessible by land and very difficult to reach by sea. This abandonment indelibly marked the city and its inhabitants. Baracoa is unique not only for historical reasons but also because of its tangible and intangible ambience. Forever present in Baracoa is the memory of the first meeting between Europeans and Amerindians.

To complete the unusual picture of the Baracoa experience, we find that, far from what would be expected, the first Cuban town is by no means colonial. Other than its fortifications, church and some of the houses, its architecture belongs to the twentieth century. In this regard, it is the most modern of the first Cuban towns. In its rural areas, however, it has conserved some archetypical examples of vernacular buildings.

BARACOA LANDSCAPE

LA SANTA CRUZ DE LA PARRA

That strange feeling of standing on the edge of post-Colombian history also has an exceptional witness: the Cruz de la Parra, the cross planted by Christopher Columbus at the Porto Santo Bay, today Baracoa Bay, on December 1, 1492. Studies aimed at proving the authenticity of such an extraordinary witness were undertaken in 1984. It was established that the cross had been made from a wood species called *Coccoloba diversifolia*, commonly known as pigeon plum and native to Central America and the Caribbean. It used to grow all over Cuba but today it can only be found in Baracoa. With the passing of time, the cross was mutilated and only part of it still remains, covered by hand-crafted silver sheets dating back to the eighteenth century. It was blessed by Pope John Paul II on his visit to Cuba in 1998.

MATACHÍN FORT

Eighteenth and Nineteenth Centuries

Museo de Historia Municipal

The experience of Jamaica captured by the English in 1655 and that of Hispaniola, half of which went to the French who founded Saint Domingue in 1681, made it advisable for Baracoa to be fortified. Its isolation at the far eastern end of Cuba made it an easy and tempting prey. From 1739 to 1742, the first defensive trenches were set up at four strategic points on the Baracoa coastline: Majana (Matachín), Punta de Esteban, La Punta and Seboruco. Shortly thereafter, engineer José Tantete, who had built the Nuestra Señora de los Ángeles Fortress on the Bay of Jagua in 1745, was sent to study a plan for the fortification of the Baracoa coast. Between 1760 and 1762, the trenches were replaced with batteries that soon became useless. They were completed and reinforced during the early nineteenth century and expanded during the second half of that century.

FRENCH COFFEE PLANTATIONS IN THE EASTERN REGION

The turmoil generated by the Revolution of the French colony of Saint Domingue brought to Cuba numerous Franco-Haitian families who settled preferably in the eastern region of the country where they promoted the cultivation of coffee during the early decades of the nineteenth century. Due to the difficult mountainous topography where they established their farms, they are considered a paradigm of human ingenuity and will.

The coffee plantations ruins represent an invaluable testimony of Caribbean plantation architecture. They are the only survivors of the type of housing that existed in Haiti and subsequently disappeared with the Revolution.

LA FRATERNIDAD

Early Nineteenth Century

Ramón de las Yaguas, Santiago de Cuba

The coffee plantation homes built by the French-Haitians were Creole exponents resulting from blending elements of Spanish, French and English architecture, all closely connected within the region. Surrounded by gardens which the homes were a part of, the most remarkable of these houses were big, two-story, rectangular buildings without courtyards, a part of which was used as the family residence and another part as warehouse or for other purposes.

Roofs were very steep: hipped with two slopes in the less complex examples, and four slopes in the larger buildings. Unlike the Spanish-style framework, the lean-to roof was not used; instead the beam covering the porch or the balcony would be supported on the lower third of the rafters that make up the framework for the main area, which is hidden from view by a flat ceiling. This created an attic which was used as storage. Originally, these roofs were covered with wooden shingles called "tejamani" (roofing boards) but because of how easily this material deteriorated in the damp conditions of the mountains, they were replaced with zinc sheets called "galvanized shingles."

The French were noted for building complicated facilities, such as aqueducts, dams and reservoirs that ensured the essential supply of water for processing coffee. They were also famous for the road network they made through the mountains.

LA ISABELICA

Early Nineteenth Century

Gran Piedra, Santiago de Cuba

The interiors of the homes were organized around a grand salon divided by wooden arches, a solution that can be seen in houses in Louisiana plantations and in house interiors in New Orleans and other U.S. cities that had ties with the French. The bedrooms would open onto the salon, while kitchens, typically, were not located inside the houses.

Load-bearing walls were masonry and the dividing walls were made of wood. The walls were structured in the way that was peculiar to the French—also used in Brazilian plantation homes—called bricks between posts or masonry between posts, consisting of a framework of sticks, placing among them a diagonal beam that affords greater strength to the wall. A horizontal piece of timber distributed throughout the window bay determined the size of the window and provided a latching device at the same time.

On one of the façades, the house is opened up with spacious balconies or porches in the case of single-level examples. Porches and balconies are supported by wooden posts, similar to those found in Santiago de Cuba homes. They are protective shields against the sun and provide vantage points for delighting in the wonderful natural surroundings where they are located.

FRENCH COFFEE PLANTATIONS IN WESTERN CUBA

French coming from Saint Domingue, from the southern United States and from France also set up plantations in the central and western parts of Cuba. Because of their singular architecture, the coffee plantation houses built by émigrés from Europe in the Sierra del Rosario are truly outstanding. In some of them, they used building solutions that were suitable for cold climates, such as thick stone walls lined with wood and steeply sloping roofs with clay-made "beaver tail" tiles. These kinds of elements had little impact as they were unsuitable for the region's intense rainfall. They remain as solitary insertions that had no continuity.

LA BELLA VISTA

Early Nineteenth Century

Sierra del Rosario, Artemisa

The dwelling house of La Bella Vista plantation is located at the top of a mountain, looking out onto a beautiful panorama, yet often hidden by clouds. Stone walls in full sight, lined with wood on the inside to conserve ambient heat, high ceilings fit for cold climates to facilitate snowfall but of little use in our environment, were unsuccessful peculiarities given their little advantage in the tropical rainy climate prevailing in the region. However, this house is a beautiful example that has been carefully restored along with the remains of the plantation.

ANGERONA

Early Nineteenth Century

Sierra del Rosario, Artemisa

The dwelling house of the Angerona coffee plantation is the typical residence found in plantations developed by the French in the Caribbean and southern United States. This dwelling model was inspired by Diego Columbus' palace (1512), built in the city of Santo Domingo. Based on that distant antecedent, the open portals feature arches supported by elegant columns, which situated on each side of the rectangle that is the house proper, allow to gaze at the surrounding scenery that is closely linked to the architectural structure.

This site, which is in ruins, holds important remains of what was once one of the wealthiest plantations in the country. The coffee plantation was promoted by the French-German Cornelio Souchay, together with his beloved Ursula Lambert, a slave from Saint Domingue. Their love for each other, which went beyond the prejudices of the time, has given Angerona a romantic and timeless connotation.

PINAR DEL RÍO AND VALLE DE VIÑALES

The city of Pinar del Río was founded over an old tobacco farming settlement in 1773. From an urban point of view, the city was organized around the course of an old roadway that crosses it from one end to the other, to which a rather regular layout was attached. Because of its distance from shipping ports, the city's growth was very slow. By the mid-nineteenth century, it barely had 100 houses and almost all of them were lean-tos or made of mud. The city became consolidated in the urban and architectural aspects in the second half of the nineteenth century when porches supported by round columns began to be attached to the facades of homes and other buildings. Pinar del Río became one of Cuba's most typical cities with porches—you can walk along the streets and be protected from both sun and rain. In the twentieth century, porches multiplied and acquired great importance.

PINAR DEL RÍO CATHEDRAL

Building on this structure, which was intended for the main parish church, began in 1880 to replace an earlier one that had been destroyed by an earthquake. It was completed in 1897, and in 1903 it was elevated to the rank of cathedral. It is a project of an academic nature presenting great verticality due to the height of the frontispiece, which, in the manner of a small temple, presides the façade. The sensation of height is emphasized by the towers on both sides. The church is an example of the architectural trend towards exaggerated height in buildings at the end of the nineteenth century.

JHS
1883

VALLE DE VIÑALES

Located in the Sierra de los Órganos near the city of Pinar del Río, the Viñales Valley is famous for its unique landscape of mogotes—isolated, steep-sided hills that rise sharply from the ground with unusually shaped silhouettes. Because of its natural merits, Viñales was included on the list of Cuban Natural Parks in 1999 and was declared by UNESCO a World Natural Heritage Site. The small farming town of Viñales has late nineteenth- and early twentieth-century traditional wooden houses with tile roofs and front porches. The valley is also noted for authentic examples of the unique vernacular architecture in the area.

BOHÍOS AND COUNTRY HOUSES

When the Spanish chronicler Gonzalo Fernández de Oviedo characterized the dwellings of pre-Hispanic peoples in the Antilles, he described two types: the circular hut called caney used by most of the natives and rectangular huts used by the tribal chieftains. Fernández de Oviedo called both types bohíos, a term that has served to identify the vernacular buildings in the region. In the beginning, the word bohío was used only for the peculiar Indian huts. The dwellings of the Spanish were called wooden houses, which were built using suitable tools for cutting wood as well as steel nails to hold down the planks. These wooden houses predominated during the early stages of development of the island's towns and coexisted with the houses constructed with finer materials.

From the seventeenth century, it was common to build walls of embarrado, a term referring to walls made of raw earth mixed with plant matter and held together by wooden posts and a crisscross framework of sticks. The embarrado technique, called bahareque in the northern regions of South America and quincha in the Southern Cone, has been associated with pre-Hispanic building traditions, although earth buildings go back to the dawn of civilization and so were known to all peoples in the history of the world.

The presence of bohíos—made either of wooden planks or earthen walls—in rural areas increased as the forms of extensive territorial ownership of the early centuries changed to smallholdings, especially tobacco farms and mills that were springing up around rivers since time immemorial. Gradually, bohíos became peasant homes par excellence. Nowadays, both types of bohíos (see below and on the following pages), with planks or earthen walls, are still around in the countryside, using roofs of guano (dry palm leaves), tiles, zinc or other more modern solutions.

ACKNOWLEDGMENTS

We wish to thank all the staff of the public and religious institutions mentioned in this book, as well as the owners of the homes depicted here for the help provided to us. We also wish to acknowledge the support given to us by Dr. Eusebio Leal, Office of the Historian of Havana; Architect Irán Millán, Office of the Conservator of Cienfuegos; María Antonieta Margolles, Historian of Sancti Spíritus; Architect Reynaldo González, Office of the Conservator of Remedios; José Rodríguez, Office of the Historian of Camagüey; Architect Omar López, Office of the Conservator of Santiago de Cuba; and Alejandro Hartman, Historian of Baracoa. Likewise, we wish to thank the staff of the following institutions: the National Archives of Cuba, in particular Jorge Macle, Director of the Map Library; the National Library of Cuba; the Archive and Library of the Office of the City Historian, Old Havana; the Provincial Historic Archive of Matanzas; and the Historical Archives of Trinidad.

Our thanks to Professor Chip Cooper of the University of Alabama at Tuscaloosa for his support, and our sincere gratitude to the John Simon Guggenheim Memorial Foundation and the Getty Conservation Institute for their assistance in the making of this book. A very special thanks to David Morton, Associate Publisher at Rizzoli International Publications, whose interest has made this book possible. Also to the editorial team in the person of Douglas Curran and his collaborators.

BIBLIOGRAPHY

Academia Española. *Diccionario de la lengua castellana* (Dictionary of the Spanish Language). 9th ed. Madrid: Imprenta de D. Francisco María Fernández, 1843.

Angulo Iñiguez, Diego. *Planos de Monumentos arquitectónicos de América y Filipinas existentes en el Archivo de Indias* (Drawings of Architectural Monuments in the Americas and the Philippines Held in the Archive of the Indies). Seville: Laboratorio de Arte, 1939.

Archivo de Indias. Ingenieros cubanos, siglos XVI, XVII y XVIII. Noticias históricas extractadas por el capitán de Ingenieros Don Benito León y Canales con notas histórico-biográficas por el Dr. Manuel Pérez Beato (Archive of the Indies. Cuban engineers, Sixteenth, Seventeenth and Eighteenth Centuries. Historical Information Excerpted by Captain of Engineers Don Benito-León y Canales with Biographical and Historical Notes by Dr. Manuel Pérez Beato). Havana: Ediciones del Archivo Histórico Pérez-Beato, 1941.

Arquitectura en Al Andalus (Architecture in Al Andalus). Lunwerg Editores, S.A., 1992.

Arrate, José Martín Félix. *Llave del Nuevo Mundo, antemural de las Indias Occidentales. La Habana descripta: noticias de su fundación, aumentos y estados* (Key to the New World, Bulwark of the West Indies. Havana Described: News of its Foundation, Increases and Situation). Havana: UNESCO Cuban Commission, 1964.

Bacardí y Moreau, Emilio. *Crónicas de Santiago de Cuba* (Chronicles of Santiago de Cuba). Barcelona: Tipografía de Carbonell y Esteva, 1908.

Barraqué, Leonor. "Santa María del Rosario y sus valores artísticos" (Santa María del Rosario and its Artistic Values) Unidentified source. 1932

Bedoya Pereda, Francisco. *La Habana desaparecida* (Lost Havana). Havana: Ediciones Boloña, 2008.

Benjamin, Asher. *The American Builder's Companion; or a System of Architecture Particularly Adapted to the Present Style of Building.* Boston: R.P. & C. Williams, 1827.

Bonet Correa, Antonio. *Andalucía barroca, arquitectura y urbanismo* (Baroque Andalusia, Architecture and Urbanism). Barcelona: Ediciones Polígrafa, S.A.

Guía de arquitectura y paisaje. An Architectural and Landscape Guide. Seville-Camagüey: Junta de Andalucía, 2009.

Contreras, Juan, Marquis of Lozoya. *Historia del arte hispánico* (History of Hispanic Art), vol. 5. Barcelona: Salvat Editores, S.A., 1931–1949.

Cornide Hernández, María Teresa. *De la Havana de siglos y de familias* (Havana of Centuries and Families). Havana: Ciencias Sociales, 2008.

Cuadro estadístico de la siempre fiel Isla de Cuba correspondiente al año de 1846 formado bajo la dirección y protección del Escmo. Sr. Gobernador y Capitán General don Leopoldo O-Donnell, por una comisión de oficiales y empleados particulares (Statistical Chart of the ever- faithful Island of Cuba for the year 1846 made, under the direction and protection of His Excellency Governor and Captain General Don Leopoldo O'Donnell, by a commission composed of officers and private employees). Imprenta del Gobierno y Capitanía General por S.M., 1847.

Cuevas Toraya, Juan de las. *500 años de construcciones en Cuba* (500 Years of Construction in Cuba). Chavín, Servicios Gráficos y Editoriales, S.L., 2001.

"Diligencias seguidas por el Rector del Colegio de la Compañía de Jesús solicitando licencia para delinear la iglesia del colegio de esta ciudad [Havana] (Procedures Carried Out by the Chancellor of the Company of Jesus College Applying for a License to Draft the School of this City [Havana]), *Boletín del Archivo Nacional,* Sep-Dec, 1914, pp. 241–264.

El mudéjar iberoamericano, del Islam al Nuevo Mundo (The Iberoamerican Mudéjar, from Islam to the New World). Barcelona: Lunwerg Editores, S.A., 1995.

Fernández, Abel: "Evolución urbana de la ciudad de La Habana durante su época colonial" (Urban Evolution of the City of Havana During the Colonial Period) *Revista del Colegio de Ingenieros Civiles de Cuba*, Havana: June 6, 1955, pp. 438–577.

Fernández y Galera, Amparo. *Cultura y costumbres en Puerto Príncipe siglos XVI-XVII* (Culture and Customs in Puerto Príncipe Sixteenth-Seventeenth Centuries). Camagüey: Editorial Ácana, 2005.

Floirián Floirián, José Enrique, and Fabrián Quintero Machado. *Baracoa a través de su historia urbana y arquitectónica* (Baracoa Through its Urban and Architectural History). Quebec: St. Augustine-Baracoa Friendship Association, 2011.

García Santana, Alicia: *Las primeras villas de Cuba* (The First Towns in Cuba). Seville: Ediciones Polymita, 2008.

———. *Matanzas, la Atenas de Cuba* (Matanzas, the Athens of Cuba). Seville: Ediciones Polymita, 2009.

———. *Urbanismo y arquitectura de la Habana Vieja, siglos XVI al XVIII* (Town Planning and Architecture of Old Havana, Sixteenth–Eighteenth Centuries). Havana: Ediciones Boloña, 2010.

———. *Trinidad de Cuba, un don del cielo* (Trinidad of Cuba, a Gift from Heaven). Madrid: Ediciones Polymita, 2010.

———. *Treinta maravillas del patrimonio arquitectónico cubano* (Thirty Wonders of Cuban Architectural Heritage). Madrid: Ediciones Polymita, 2012.

Gómez Consuegra, Lourdes. "Santa María del Puerto del Príncipe. Una irregular villa colonial de Cuba. Análisis del surgimiento de la hoy ciudad de Camagüey referido desde la perspectiva arquitectónica de su trazado" (Santa María del Puerto del Príncipe: An Irregular Cuban Colonial Town. Analysis of the Creation of Today's City of Camagüey from the Architectural Perspective of its Layout), *Senderos, Revista de la Oficina del Historiador de la ciudad de Camagüey*, No. 0, pp. 10–14.

Guarch Delmonte, José M. "Sitio arqueológico El Chorro de Maíta" (El Chorro de Maíta Archeological Site), *Revista Cubana de Ciencias Sociales*, May-Aug, 1988, pp. 162–184.

Habana antigua. Apuntes históricos por el Dr. Manuel Pérez-Beato (Old Havana: Historical Notes by Dr. Manuel Pérez-Beato), vol. I. Havana: Seoane, Fernández y Ca., 1936.

Henares Cuéllar, Ignacio, and Rafael López Guzmán. *Arquitectura mudéjar granadina* (Mudéjar Architecture in Granada). Granada, 1989.

Herrera López, Pedro A. "De los orígenes de la ciudad y de la iglesia de Santa María del Rosario" (On the Origins of the City and the Santa María del Rosario Church), *Palabra Nueva*. Havana: October 1998, pp. 14–16.

———. "La casa de la Obrapía" (The House of Pious Works), *Palabra* Nueva. Havana: October, 2000, pp. 40–42.

———. *Tres personajes de la Noble Habana* (Three Figures from Noble Havana). Havana: Letras Cubanas, 2005.

Hill, Robert. *Cuba and Porto Rico with Other Islands of the West Indies.* New York: The Century Co., 1898.

Jiménez Margolles, María A. et al. *Monumentos*

nacionales y locales de Sancti Spíritus (National and Local Monuments in Sancti Spíritus). Sancti Spíritus: Ediciones Jarao, 2003.

La Habana Vieja. Mapas y planos en los archivos de España (Old Havana: Maps and Drawings in the Spanish Archives). Madrid: Ministerio de Asuntos Exteriores de España, Ministerio de Cultura de España, Ministerio de Cultura de Cuba, 1985.

La Habana. Guía de arquitectura/Havana. Cuba. *An Architectural Guide*. Research, selection, catalog and texts by María Elena Martin Zequeira and Eduardo Rodriguez Fernández. Havana-Seville: Junta de Andalucía, 1998.

Lapique Becali, Zoila. *La memoria en las piedras* (The memory on the stones). Havana: Ediciones Boloña, 2002.

La visita eclesiástica (The Ecclesiastical Visit). Selection and introduction by César García del Pino. Havana: Ciencias Sociales, 1985.

Las Villas y Matanzas. Guía de arquitectura y paisaje. An Architectural and Landscape Guide. Seville-Santa Clara: Junta de Andalucía, 2012.

Le Roy y Cassá, Jorge. *Historia del hospital de San Francisco de Paula* (History of the Hospital in San Francisco de la Paula). Havana: Imprenta El Siglo XX, 1958.

Maza, Aquiles de la. *Eutimio Falla Bonet. Su obra filantrópica y la arquitectura* (Eutimio Falla Bonet. His Philanthropic Work and Architecture). Geneva, 1971.

— — —, and Raúl Macías. "La arquitectura colonial de Trinidad" (Trinidad's Colonial Architecture), *Arquitectura*. Havana: January 1939, pp. 5–17.

Miranda, Leo. "De cómo y cuando nació Santiago de Cuba para la historia" (When and How Santiago de Cuba was Born for History), *Del Caribe*, 1987, pp. 18–23.

Martín Leiseca, Juan. *Apuntes para la historia eclesiástica de Cuba* (Notes for an Ecclesiastical History of Cuba). Talleres Tipográficos de Carasa y Ca., 1938.

Marrero, Leví. *Cuba, economía y sociedad* (Cuba, Economy and Society), vol. 10. Madrid: Playor, 1972–1976.

Oriente de Cuba. *Guia de arquitectura/An Architectural Guide*. Seville, Junta de Andalucía, 2002.

Pérez Luna, Rafael Félix. *Historia de Sancti Spíritus* (History of Sancti Spíritus), vol. 2. Sancti Spíritus: La Paz, 1888.

Pezuela, Jacobo de la. *Diccionario geográfico, estadístico, histórico de la isla de Cuba* (Geographical, Statistical, Historical Dictionary of the Island of Cuba), vol. 4. Madrid: Imprenta del Banco Industrial y Mercantil, 1863–1866.

Pichardo, Hortensia. "Noticias de Cuba" (News from Cuba), *Santiago*, Santiago de Cuba: December, 1975, pp. 7–44.

— — —. *La fundación de las primeras villas de la Isla de Cuba* (The foundation of the First Towns in the Island of Cuba). Havana: Ciencias Sociales, 1986.

— — —. *Documentos para la historia de Cuba* (Documents for the History of Cuba), vol. 1. Havana: Ciencias Sociales, 1971.

Portuondo, Fernando. *El segundo viaje de descubrimiento* (The Second Journey of Discovery), Havana: Ciencias Sociales, 1977.

Prat Puig, Francisco. *El prebarroco en Cuba. Una escuela criolla de arquitectura morisca* (Pre-Baroque in Cuba. A Creole School of Mudéjar Architecture). Havana: Burgay & Cia., 1947.

— — —. "La catedral de La Habana. Bosquejo de un estudio e interpretación del monumento" (Havana Cathedral: Outline of a Study and Interpretation of the Monument), *Revista Bimestre Cubana*, January–June, 1957, pp. 36–59.

— — —. *La arquitectura colonial en Santiago de Cuba* (Colonial Architecture in Santiago de Cuba). Santiago de Cuba: Universidad de Oriente, 1963.

— — —. *La casa de Diego Velázquez y el Museo de Ambiente Histórico Cubano* (Diego Velázquez's House and the Museum of Cuban Historical Environment). Santiago de Cuba, 1972.

Ramos y Duarte, Félix. *Diccionario Yucayo etimológico histórico e ilustrado con mil doscientos grabados de pueblos de indios, lugares indígenas de aborígenes antillanos celebres, mapas de la isla con sus cacicazgos, dibujos de objetos de alfarería de minerales, plantas, frutas i animales con sus colores naturales, sus nombres indios i clarificación científica etc.* (Yucayo historical etymological dictionary illustrated with engravings of Indian villages, indigenous places of famous West Indian aborigines, maps of the island with their chiefdoms, drawings of pottery objects made of minerals, plants, fruits and animals in their natural colors, their Indian names and scientific clarification, etc.). Havana: Archivo Histórico del Museo de la Ciudad de la Oficina del Historiador de la Habana, 1919.

"Recomendaciones formuladas al comité gestor de la restauración de la iglesia Parroquial Mayor de la ciudad de Sancti Spíritus por el arq. Joaquín E. Weiss" (Recommendations made to the Committee Responsible for the Restoration of the Main Parish Church of Sancti Spíritus by the Architect Joaquín E. Weiss), *Arquitectura*, September 1952, pp. 381–388.

Rodríguez Ramos, Rafael, and Magalys Cisneros Ramírez. *Bayamo, dos espacios históricos* (Bayamo, Two Historical Spaces). Madrid: Pablo de la Torriente, 1997.

Roig de Leuchsenring, Emilio. *La plaza de Armas Carlos Manuel de Céspedes de La Habana* (Havana's Plaza de Armas Carlos Manuel de Céspedes). Havana: Junta Nacional de Arqueología y Etnología, 1957.

— — —. *La Habana-Apuntes históricos* (Havana - Historical Notes). Havana, 1939.

Romero, Leandro. *La Habana arqueológica y otros ensayos* (Archaeological Havana and Other Essays). Havana: Letras Cubanas, 1995.

Sánchez-Agusti, María. *Los edificios públicos de La Habana en el siglo XVIII* (Public Buildings in Eighteenth-Century Havana). Valladolid: Universidad de Valladolid, 1984.

Santa Cruz y Mallen, Francisco Xavier, Count of Jaruco. *Historia de familias cubanas* (Stories of Cuban Families), vol. 6. Havana: Ediciones Hércules, 1940–1950.

Solano, Francisco. *Normas y leyes de la ciudad hispanoamericana (1492–1600)* (Norms and Laws of Spanish-American Cities [1492–1600]), vol. 1. Madrid: Consejo Superior de Investigaciones Científicas, Centro de Estudios Históricos, 1996.

Tamames Henderson, Marcos. *La ciudad como texto cultural Camagüey. 1514–1837* (The City as a Cultural Text Camagüey. 1514–1837). Camagüey: Editorial Ácana, 2005.

Weiss, Joaquín. "La Catedral de la Habana. Proceso histórico-arquitectónico de su construcción y consideraciones sobre su posible autor" (Havana Cathedral: Historical and Architectural Process of its Construction and Considerations on its Possible Author), *Revista del Colegio de Arquitectos*, Havana, October 1931, pp. 44–74.

— — —. *Arquitectura cubana colonial colección de las principales y más característicos edificios erigidos en Cuba durante la dominación española, precedida de una reseña histórica arquitectónica* (Cuban colonial architecture, collection of the principal and most characteristic buildings built in Cuba during the Spanish rule, preceded by an architectural/historical review). Havana: Cultural, S.A., 1936.

— — —. *Arquitectura colonial cubana* (Cuban Colonial Architecture). Havana-Seville, Instituto Cubano del Libro-Junta de Andalucía, 2002.

Wright, Irene. *Historia documentada de San Cristóbal de La Habana en el siglo XVI* (Documented History of San Cristobal de La Habana in the Sixteenth Century), vol. 1. Havana: Imprenta El Siglo XX, MCMXXVII, 1927.

Ximeno, José Manuel. "Casas capitulares de la Habana de los siglos XVI y XVII" (Sixteenth and Seventeenth-Century Chapterhouses in Havana), *Arquitectura*, Havana, August 1939.